10 Publishing Myths

Praise for
10 Publishing Myths

"Terry Whalin has seen publishing from every possible angle and has the best practical advice any writer can get. The inside scoop."

— **Rick Hamlin**, executive editor, *Guideposts* magazine

"In my years working for publishers and now as a literary agent, I meet authors with big dreams and expectations. Some of these authors succeed with their plans while others fail. The ones who succeed have a plan. Terry Whalin pours his publishing experience into *10 Publishing Myths*. His insights will help you succeed."

— **Marilyn Allen**, President,
Allen O'Shea Literary Agency

"Terry Whalin masterfully addresses the common myths and then serves up straight talk about the publishing industry. Sharing from decades of knowledge and experience, he aptly resets expectations and speaks the truth that aspiring authors need to hear. If you believe there is a book in you, be sure to read this one so you are fully prepared to travel the way forward."

— **Tami Heim**, President and CEO,
Christian Leadership Alliance

"This book is chock-full of savvy publishing advice. I wish every writer would read this and avoid being surprised by the way things work in publishing."

— **Steve Laube**, President, The Steve Laube Agency

"I like to say, "writers write books and authors sell books". Before you take on the ambitious challenge of publishing a book, go into it with as much knowledge of this ever-changing industry as you can. Terry Whalin has seen the missteps and the success. I recommend a careful study of *10 Publishing Myths* to give your book the best possible chance to succeed."

— **Carlton Garborg**, President,
Broadstreet Publishing Group

"Terry Whalin's new book, *10 Publishing Myths, Insights Every Author Needs to Succeed,* gives authors solid action steps to take to be successful while increasing their understanding about the business of publishing. He breaks the myths that hinder authors in their journey."

— **Susan Reichert,** Editor-in-Chief,
Southern Writers Magazine.

"Every aspiring author should read Terry Whalin's *10 Publishing Myths*. Within these pages, he guides writers through the publishing process and gives them realistic expectations and a healthy dose of reality."

— **Rolf Zettersten**, 30 year publishing veteran

"*10 Publishing Myths, Insights Every Author Needs to Succeed* is not merely a collection of "tips and tricks" for writers. Based on years of inside experience, author Terry Whalin offers straight-talk advice to anyone willing to do the hard work necessary for publishing success."

— **David Horton**, Vice President Editorial,
Bethany House Publishers

"For years, so-called truths have floated around in the publishing world, and naïve writers have believed them. In *10 Publishing Myths*, Terry reveals the truth and shares important principles that affect a writer's success. Using examples and stories, he shows what works and then provides plenty of help—including action steps—to encourage writers on the right path. Terry's vast experience in the industry makes this an excellent resource."

— **Cecil Murphey**, bestselling author of 140 books,
including *90 Minutes in Heaven* (with Don Piper) and
Gifted Hands: The Ben Carson Story (with Dr. Ben Carson)

"Terry Whalin's *10 Publishing Myths: Insights Every Author Needs to Succeed* is much needed wisdom and an eye level reality check that comes from Terry's decades in the book business as a writer and working on the inside of the top publishing houses. It is both unvarnished truth and uplifting encouragement for writers and would-be writers out there, a road map of the writing business if there ever was one. I highly recommend it!"

— **Dennis R. Welch**, President, Articulate,
PR and Communications

"Essential reading for all new writers. I especially like the myth that is addressed in Chapter 4, "Beginning Writers Have No Chance to Get Published." Get ready to take notes. This could change everything for you."

— **Robin Jones Gunn**, over 5 million books sold

"Ever have one of those, "Wish I would have known!" moments? Me too. Especially at the start of my writing career. Fortunately you can know ahead of time with Terry's stellar book. He takes his extensive experience in publishing and distils it down in a way that will educate, encourage, and save you a great many detours on your path to publication."

— **James L. Rubart**, Five-time Christy Award winning author

"As a literary agent and writer who has been in the publishing industry over twenty-five years, I heartily recommend this book. I completely concur with Terry's assessment of the 10 myths because I hear them all the time from writers who contact me for help. His insights in the introduction alone are worth the price of the book, but each section offers a wealth of experience and knowledge that will save you time and frustration. If you are a writer, you definitely need this book."

— **Karen Hardin**, PriorityPR Group and Literary Agency, www.prioritypr.org

"A much-needed read providing solid, practical plans to increase the odds for success."

— **Bill Myers**, bestselling author

"Terry Whalin dispels 10 myths about the publishing world openly and honestly while sharing insights from his many years in the industry. This is a must-read for any writer, published or not, a true reality check that will tame expectations yet encourage writers to take the appropriate steps to succeed."

– **Rachelle Gardner**, Literary Agent,
Books & Such Literary Management

"A trusted voice, an experienced insider, a knowledgeable advocate for authors of all genres, this is a gift to all writers (and, yes, this IS a run-on sentence). So grab your highlighter and begin this wonderful education, complete with practical exercises."

– **Don Pape**, Publisher, NavPress

"Navigating the book publishing maze is confusing and overwhelming to many, but book pro Terry Whalin, whom I have known for over a decade, helps you to avoid the pitfalls so that your publishing experience can be powerful, positive and productive—and most importantly, a profitable one."

– **Brian Feinblum**, Chief Marketing Officer,
Media Connect, Founder of
www.BookMarketingBuzzBlog.blogspot.com

"Sound, practical advice from an industry expert. This little book will keep you from unnecessary mistakes and provide a great foundation for your writing career."

– **James Scott Bell**, International
Thriller Writers Award winner

"As an editor, I often encounter writers with high hopes that someone will help them: an agent, a publisher, a bookseller. Yet each of those roles are mostly outside the author's control. In *10 Publishing Myths*, Terry Whalin helps authors wise up to the nuances of the publishing industry and shows them how to take control of their success with hands-on action steps. Every author can benefit from reading this book—whether publishing their first book or many books."

— **Alice Crider**, Senior Acquisitions Editor,
David C. Cook

10 Publishing Myths

Insights Every Author
Needs to Succeed

W. TERRY WHALIN

NEW YORK

LONDON • NASHVILLE • MELBOURNE • VANCOUVER

10 Publishing Myths
Insights Every Author Needs to Succeed

Published in New York, New York, by Morgan James Publishing. Morgan James is a trademark of Morgan James, LLC. www.MorganJamesPublishing.com

ISBN 978-1-64279-452-6 paperback
ISBN 978-1-64279-453-3 eBook
Library of Congress Control Number: 2019900588

Cover Design by:
Rachel Lopez
www.r2cdesign.com

Interior Design by:
Bonnie Bushman
The Whole Caboodle Graphic Design

In an effort to support local communities, raise awareness and funds, Morgan James Publishing donates a percentage of all book sales for the life of each book to Habitat for Humanity Peninsula and Greater Williamsburg.

Get involved today! Visit
www.MorganJamesBuilds.com

Dedication

To the Writers and Editors Who Have Taught
Powerful Lessons During My Years in Publishing.
Thank you.

Contents

Foreword

I've enjoyed great opportunities to write and tell stories, and I live an author's dream.

While mainstream fiction is my love, for years I generated a healthy six-figure income largely by writing famous people's as-told-to autobiographies. These weren't ghost jobs. My name appeared on the covers of books I wrote for superstar athletes like Hank Aaron, Walter Payton, Meadowlark Lemon, Nolan Ryan, Joe Gibbs, and more. I wrote books for BJ Thomas and Bill Gaither and even for evangelists like Billy Graham and Luis Palau.

At the same time, I worked a day job as a magazine publisher and editor, and later I ran a major Inspirational market book publishing house. Knowing from experience what I faced from people like me—gatekeepers for magazines and books—I took a disciplined approach to my own freelancing. I knew what editors really thought of sloppy—and/or late—work. Our letters to would-be authors were cordial, but having been on the editorial side of the desk, I determined to avoid the freelance writer's usual reputation. (For one thing, I learned that only one of a hundred writers literally make their deadlines.)

Sorry to break it to you, but behind closed doors, editors say things you wouldn't want to hear. To cut the tension, they would occasionally add scathing comments to evaluation sheets meant only for colleagues' eyes. They could be humorously, but brutally, honest.

The world of book publishing is ever changing. Books and publishers appear with great success and then disappear. Editors and agents change companies. In our digital age, everything is faster, more direct, seemingly easier. I'm old enough to remember buying manuscript boxes and packing up my precious babies to ship to publishers. Today, I attach my manuscripts to emails and transmit them in seconds. With the advent of print-on-demand and seemingly miraculous printing technology, anyone can be printed—in hard copies or on the Internet—and call it publishing.

But the old rules still apply. Be sure to exhibit the same professionalism sending electronic documents as you did using snail mail. I'm appalled at how punctuation and spelling seem to have been abandoned for the sake of speed, and often it appears writers are making up rules as they go along. I strive to make sure that anything I write, even a brief note—and boy can they be brief—is spelled and punctuated correctly.

Especially when communicating with editors, publishers, and agents, your prospects for success depend on how you come across. Leave nothing to chance. Quality and timing trump quantity.

In 1995 I began writing the *Left Behind* novel series, which has sold over 60 million copies. Today this series continues to sell around 10,000 units each month. What most people don't realize is that *Left Behind* was my 125th published book. Some overnight success, eh?

Tyndale House took a big risk by releasing *Left Behind* in hardcover—rarely done back then in the Inspirational market. So to hedge their bet on the success of the novel, because book jackets cost as much as the actual book, Tyndale printed thirty-five thousand books, but just twenty thousand jackets. If the book didn't sell, they could shred the remainders and save the expense of printing more jackets.

During its first year of release, *Left Behind* sold nearly ninety thousand hardbacks, and the rest is history. But that careful strategy shows the risk inherent with every book released into the marketplace.

Working with thousands of would-be authors through my Jerry Jenkins Writers Guild, I understand writers' dreams and ambitions for their books. Some dreams are just that—pure fantasy not grounded in the reality of the book publishing business. I think it's important that writers like you know the truth from the beginning. And that's why I'm enthusiastic about *10 Publishing Myths* and recommend it to all my Guild members.

I've known Terry Whalin since our days as magazine editors decades ago, and we've interacted at Evangelical Press Association meetings and shared the platform at countless writers conferences. Terry is a skilled writer in addition to having been a magazine editor, book editor, and literary agent. He has worked with many authors and seen books both succeed and flop.

Terry takes his years in publishing and pours all he's learned into this practical volume. Every chapter is filled with insights, stories, and action steps you can take. He teaches that the business aspects are as important as the creative side of publishing. If your book doesn't have an eye-catching title and cover, you'll have trouble gaining traction with bookstore owners and their customers—let alone potential readers from all the online venues.

But if you follow Terry's advice, you'll give your book the best opportunity for success. His easy-to-apply ideas offer the resources you need.

—Jerry B. Jenkins
JerryJenkins.com
JerrysGuild.com

Introduction

You and I are living in an incredible time of history. Most of us carry a powerful device in our pocket called a Smartphone—an amazing communication tool. No matter where we are in the world, we can receive emails or use social media like Facebook or Twitter to reach others in an instant. It has never been easier to get published—books, magazine articles, blog posts, videos and any number of other ways.

Each of these tools is a far cry from where I began my career in publishing—sitting at the typewriter. The typewriter has no feature to save your writing or correct your spelling. The skill of typing which I learned in high school had incredible value to me. I began to write stories in my head and compose them sitting at the typewriter. The ability to write a story was more difficult when you had to use a typewriter. My high school English teacher, Mr. Smith, saw some writing ability in my work and encouraged me to join the school newspaper. Although not athletic or interested in sports, I wrote what they needed: sports. I learned how to write a headline and interesting opening paragraph. I began to learn the language and cadence of storytelling.

While each of us writes our stories for ourselves, I learned how to focus on the expectations of the reader as I worked on my high school newspaper. While working with others, I gained an appreciation for the role of the editor to give feedback and improve the story as well as guidance on what worked for the publication. Every publication has a unique target reader and as a writer, you need to develop and hone this skill to reach a particular audience.

As you tell your story, the printed page has incredible power to change lives. I've seen this power firsthand in my own life. In the early days of my college life, I was rebelling from my upbringing and joined a social fraternity with an active party lifestyle drinking alcohol. As a part of my college experience, I was searching for truth and the meaning of life. I found a partial answer in purchasing a book called *Jesus the Revolutionary*. I wondered, *how could Jesus be a revolutionary?* This book revealed the reality of Jesus and my life changed. From reading this book, my plans changed and I spent 10 years in linguistics instead of chasing stories through journalism. Eventually I returned to my writing life and my stories have been published in over 50 magazines and I've written more than 60 books for traditional publishers. I've spent 25+ years in the world of publishing which is full of possibilities with each opportunity.

Yet with the explosion of possibilities, there are also many publishing myths or misconceptions that can snare aspiring writers. No matter how authors publish, the bottom-line goal is <u>successful publishing</u> and gaining readers. You can slave and craft your words and put them out into the world but if only a few (or no one) reads them, then you have committed a colossal waste of your time and energy. If I mention information more than once, it is to emphasize the importance of certain facts. As you grasp these facts, it will increase your chance of being published and selling books.

Numerous publishing myths snare writers to lead them down the wrong path. In the following pages, I've selected 10 of the biggest ones to dispel. My hope is the stories combined with the call to action at the end of each chapter will provide you a roadmap to succeed with your writing.

Chapter 1

Myth One

I Will Make a Lot of Money Writing My Book

Whenever you tell a certain story, friends and family have responded, "That story would make a great book." Or "You should write a book about that." You've listened to the encouragement of others and now you wonder if maybe you *should* write this book. Because you have a computer, you put your fingers on the keyboard and with great passion, you begin to write your book.

You are not alone in such an experience. It is mirrored thousands of times with others. Publishing experts guess that at any given time, over a million manuscripts and proposals are circulating in different offices and agencies. Which ones will get published and succeed?

One of the greatest publishing myths I've encountered is the belief "my book will make a lot of money." Over the years, I've met many passionate writers. One brand new writer told me, "My book is going to be a bestseller." This confident boast intrigued me and I wanted to know more details such as the focus of the book and the publisher. When the author said, "Balboa Press" I knew this author was headed for a rude awakening. Balboa Press is a self-publishing company and a part of Author Solutions. From my years in publishing, I knew this company was going to publish close to 50,000 titles this year. For this author to break out with a bestseller would be nearly impossible. To become a bestseller, the book needs broad distribution to online plus brick and mortar bookstores who report their sales to a bestseller list. Balboa Press is online and their books are not sold in brick and mortar bookstores. Also with the large volume of titles each year, it is common publishing knowledge that the bulk of Author Solutions (and Balboa Press) employees are in the Philippines. I've seen a number of books from these publishers and their covers are poor (Good covers sell books). The overall production of these books is not good quality. I hoped this author didn't spend a lot of money to produce her book. I've met authors who have a garage full of books from these companies and have spent $20,000 to produce them (no exaggeration). It is heart breaking to witness such scams and authors need to be careful.

To ensure publishing success, avoid using the wrong publisher. Here are three steps to help you sort good from bad:

Use Google to see what is online. Type: Publisher name + complaint then read a page or two of the entries. Are the complaints new or old? Are there many entries or a few?

1. A reality of the internet is every publisher has complaints and anyone can write anything and give a one-sided story. These comments stay online forever.
2. Speak with some of the publishers' authors and ask about their experiences.
3. Read and get professional help on the contract. Make sure you understand it.

These actions will help you avoid many publishing pitfalls.

According to some publishing professionals there are over 4,500 new books published *every day*. This statistic includes self-published and traditional published books. It has never been easier to create a book. The challenge for every author is to actually <u>sell</u> books and make money from them.

While this chapter is focused on the myth that you will make a lot of money writing your book, let's be honest. There are several other important reasons to write a book:

1. When you publish a book, it validates your expertise and knowledge in a particular area. Because you've written a book, you have become an "expert" who is respected and asked to speak to others in this area.
2. If your book is tied to your current business, the book can become a "calling card" that you use to get additional leads, sales and business for your company.
3. Passion for a topic drives your book. Besides making money, many writers have a message they want to get out into the world. A well-written book can add to your authority and credibility as it is published and reaches the audience.

As you publish a book, many of the details related to money from the book are outside of the author's control. Your author earnings depend on how you publish (traditional, hybrid or self-publish). In addition, what you have negotiated in your contract for your ability to purchase the books as an author affects your bottom-line. Another important factor related to money is what you and your publisher create for the book in terms of cover design, availability of the book in the bookstore (distribution) and many other details.

The publisher you select has a lot to do with getting your book into the right places online and in physical bookstores. Some authors believe they can make money if their book is on Amazon. While Amazon is a large part of the book selling market, there are many other online bookstores and places that people buy books: bookstores, airports, grocery stores and much more. You want your book to be in the broadest possible number of places to succeed, sell and make money. The publisher controls much of this distribution.

Another important money making detail relates to every book inside your local bookstore. The books are there on consignment. The retailer can return the books to the publisher for a full refund for the lifetime of the book if the book does not sell. The publisher takes all of the risk on the books inside the bookstore—yet it is the author's marketing and activity that drives bookstore sales. Everyone must work together to sell books and make money.

Because many of these financial details are outside of your control as an author, what steps can you take? From my 25+ years in publishing, I've observed that selling books does not occur without the author taking action. The great showman P.T. Barnum once said, "Without promotion, something terrible happens. Nothing." No matter whether a major publisher releases your book or you self-publish, as the author you will bear the bulk of the responsibility to market your book. If they are honest no author wants to spend the time-consuming and difficult task to market their book.

They would rather delegate this marketing responsibility to someone else.

One of the most successful series of books in the English language is *Chicken Soup for the Soul*. During the launch of the first book, authors Jack Canfield and Mark Victor Hansen followed a principle they called The Rule of Five. Every day these authors took five actions to promote their book. They gave a radio interview. They wrote a guest blog post. They posted on Facebook and secured an interview with a newspaper. The fact they took five actions every day to promote their book paid off. They met their goals and the books sold and they became famous.

Chicken Soup for the Soul didn't start that way. Health Communications International published the first book, which was a small unknown publisher in Florida. Jack Canfield and Mark Victor Hansen told their publisher they were going to sell a million books in the first year. Their publisher laughed at them. At that point, the authors had never sold a million copies of any book and it looked impossible. Yet Canfield and Hansen were determined with their Big Hairy Audacious Goal and it took them a year and a half to reach a million copies of sold books. Consider what steps you can take with your book to follow their example related to the rule of five.

The path to becoming a bestseller is different for each author. If we had an exact formula in this process, <u>every</u> book would be a bestseller—and every book is not a bestseller.

What can you do as an author to ensure your success and the money-making potential with your book?

One of my favorite books is *The Success Principles* by Jack Canfield. I've read this book several times and I've also listened to this entire book on audio. Canfield has spent a lifetime studying the principles that people follow to be successful. I want you to be successful as an author. The first and the most important principle in the book says, "Take 100% Responsibility for Your Life."

This principle applies to the constant wish for every author to have someone else market your book. Are you reaching out to your target audience? Have you identified your target audience for your book? Where are they and how are you reaching out to touch them on a consistent basis? It does not have to be daily but it does have to be regular. Give them great content on your topic and in that process point them to more information inside your book.

One of the best ways for you to take responsibility is to create your own marketing plans. Whether you self-publish or have a traditional publisher to get your book into the bookstore, these plans are important. Whether your book is launching soon or has been out for a while, you need to be creating and executing your own marketing plans (More detail about this factor will appear later in the book).

I assume you are reading this book because you want to make money with your book. While there are many factors outside of your control as an author, there is one person you can control—you. Your attitude and commitment to marketing your book is critical.

Most authors approach publishing as a creative endeavor (which it is) and they neglect the business details of publishing. The myths in this book come from this neglect of the business aspects. At the conclusion of each chapter, I've added a specific action you can take as author to counteract the myth in your publishing life. If you follow these action steps, it is as though you are earning your MBA—no not a Masters in Business Administration. I'm using MBA as an abbreviation for **Myth Buster Action**.

 Myth Buster Action (MBA): a mental attitude shift can be one of the most important learning tools for every author. Take 100% responsibility as an author to sell books.

Chapter 2

Myth Two

My Publisher Will
Sell and Promote My Book

In 2007, America's Publicist Rick Frishman called and invited me to participate on the faculty of MegaBook Marketing University in Los Angeles, California. At that time, I was running a small literary agency and representing authors in Scottsdale, Arizona. Mark Victor Hansen, co-author of *Chicken Soup for the Soul* was leading this event. Besides meeting with authors who pitched their books, I attended every single session of the event and took notes. Throughout these sessions, I learned that traditional publishers are skilled at making beautiful books with well-designed covers and interiors. Book publishers also know how to get the books inside the bookstore and available to the public.

My first book, a children's picture book for David C. Cook, was published in 1992. Since then I had written over 50 books with traditional publishers, received a couple of six-figure advances yet most of my books had negative royalty statements. A little known but important publishing fact is ninety percent of nonfiction books never earn back their advance. All my books are nonfiction.

While I loved writing books, I did very little promotion for my work. I had a small website (www.terrywhalin.com) but I had not blogged and had no social media presence or email list or consistent and on-going connections to my readers. I believed because I was working with traditional publishers, receiving an advance against my royalties (sometimes thousands of dollars) that my books were going to be selling. I had fallen for the myth expressed in this chapter that my publisher was going to promote and sell my book.

During MegaBook Marketing University, I learned a key truth about publishing: publishers know how to make beautiful books and get them into bookstores yet these actions are only one part of the process. The other key element (mostly up to the author) is actually selling the book to the consumer. Attending MegaBook Marketing

University transformed my life. I could no longer assume the responsibility for selling my books would be in the hands of the publisher (or someone else besides me). I made a decision to change and take action.

Every writer needs to be able to tell stories and create an excellent book manuscript. The writing is a foundational skill for every writer. If you don't have this writing skill, a developmental editor, ghostwriter, co-author or any other person in this role can help you create an engaging book. But marketing and selling your book requires a different set of skills. The good news is **every writer can learn to market their book**.

Many writers want to sprint to the finish line complete their book then push it into the market. I've found most authors have the wrong mental picture of the process. Instead of a sprint, publishing is more like a marathon. Slow, steady and consistent action will get you your audience and success. Your book doesn't fly into the market but slow and steady sales and marketing will help your audience make a buying decision, know about the book, then buy and read the book. Finally you want your audience to love the information or story in your book so that they enthusiastically tell others about your book and increase your audience and sales.

Writers are looking for a simple formula to sell books. If such a formula existed, then publishers would use this method and every book would make a lot of money. In fact, some unexpected books are hits while some well-written books do not get purchased. One of the keys to selling books is building relationships. John Kremer, the author of *1001 Ways to Market Your Book* says marketing is about building relationships with your readers.

Consider your reader or target audience. How much detail do you know about them? Where do they live? Where do they shop? What other books do they read? Are they active in book clubs? What are their needs and how can you write material that will meet those needs? Can you answer these and other audience questions?

When it comes to book marketing, it is easy to fall into "shiny object syndrome." Every week a new social network launches and is the latest place for you to find readers. Snapchat is booming and people will say you have to be active on this network. Or because everyone is spending time on Facebook, you must be active on this platform. Before you jump and spend a lot of money and energy, ask: "Do I own the platform?" No. Facebook, Twitter or Instagram is all "rented" space. You can be banned or kicked off this space because you do not own it. You do not want to invest a lot of effort into building your audience on a rented space. But if you do use Twitter, Facebook or Instagram, understand the potential risks.

One of the most effective tools for every book author is to create their own email list. As an author, you control your email list including what you say and how often you use the list. While not everyone looks at Facebook or a website or Twitter, most people open and read their email. If you email too frequently, they might not open your email or they might unsubscribe. When an author has an email list and uses it properly, it is the best way for them to reach their readers. If you are a brand new author, how do you start a list and use it effectively?

My email list's audience is focused on individuals interested in writing books or magazine articles (publishing). I have a number of "list building" devices that encourage people to subscribe to my email list. For example, I wrote the Ebook, *Straight Talk from the Editor, 18 Keys to a Rejection-proof Submission*. This Ebook is available at: www. StraightTalkEditor.com. If you go to this site, you will see that I make it easy for you to get my book—but you have to give me your first name and email address. This means you have been added to my personal email list. Every author needs to give away an Ebook or audio or video to entice their audience to join their email list. If someone does not want to be on my list, every email gives them a simple way to unsubscribe. Each time I send a mailing to my list, people unsubscribe and that is OK. Sometimes their needs have changed and they are no longer interested. You want readers who are on your list and committed to reading your emails.

Every author can create a free Ebook related to their book. Here's some of the steps in this process:

1. Identify your target reader. You should know this reader already from writing your book. What types of subscribers do you want to attract? Write this element down and the more specific you can be, the better the identification process.

2. Brainstorm what this reader needs and their desires. Listing the possibilities will help you clarify the type of Ebook you should create and its specific content. As with the previous step, write down these needs so you have a thoughtful list.

3. With the specific audience and their needs, you are ready to write your Ebook. Before you spend a lot of time creating original work, do you already have some of the content in another form? Maybe you have written some magazine articles that could become a series of chapters in your Ebook. Or maybe you have a blog with entries and can take some of these entries and organize them into a series of chapters for your Ebook. For many years, I've been creating original content however there is wisdom in repurposing content you have already created. Your Ebook should be long enough to create value for your reader. I suggest the finished Ebook be at least 20 to 30 pages. In your Ebook you are focused on creating something of value. It is critical this Ebook be targeted to your audience and provide content that they want from you. As an alternative giveaway,

you can also create a 30 to 45 minute audiobook file which can become your giveaway.

4. After you have written your Ebook, create a PDF. As a part of this process, I encourage you to get a simple cover designed for the PDF. This cover can be designed by someone through Fiverr.com for about $5. Look through the different vendors and select someone with good ratings. Then reach out to them through Fiverr to get your cover created. After the cover is made, you can use it to create an image which you can use in the marketing of the Ebook. Or if you don't want to use Fiverr, I recommend you get a set of PDF templates. I have used one called Easy PDF templates because it gave me a lot of options and was an inexpensive way to create these Ebooks.

As an author, you take control of what you can for your book. You cannot depend on your publisher to sell your book. You have the greatest passion for your book so you need to show that passion and create an email list and different ways to connect with your readers.

 Myth Buster Action (MBA): Create a free book then use this Ebook to begin your own email list. Use a simple or free program like Mail Chimp or Constant Contact. Create it today and then begin using it on a regular basis.

Chapter 3

Myth Three

Writing a Book
Will Make Me Famous

Many writers believe writing a book will make them famous. They believe writing the book and getting it into the market will make them well-known. This idea is a publishing myth. As I've detailed in chapter 1, without the author's promotion, something terrible happens—nothing. What are you doing to increase your connection to your audience?

Within the publishing community, the buzz word is "platform." Agents and editors will ask writers, "Tell me about your platform." In a speaking arena, a platform is a raised section and where the speaker talks to be visible and reach his audience. The word platform is a way of asking about your audience and your connections. There are many ways to build or have a platform. It could be through a social media site like Facebook, LinkedIn or Twitter. An author can have similar or different connections on each of these networks. While there is no perfect number for these networks, the larger the better.

My encouragement to you in the platform area is to have real numbers and not fake ones. A year or two ago, one of my journalist friends had a major publisher releasing her new book. I knew she had a small Twitter following yet one day I saw she had gone from a small following of hundreds to over 100,000. The sudden increase was suspicious because anyone can go to a website and purchase 100,000 followers. When you "buy" followers, your numbers certainly increase but they are not real followers who engage with you and actually buy your books.

As an example, I have over 200,000 followers on Twitter which is an aspect of my market platform. This platform did not happen overnight. I've been on Twitter since 2009 and steadily building my audience. People follow me for several reasons. First, I give varied and targeted content for my audience. I also tweet 12-15 times throughout a day. My tweets point to additional information and each one includes an image for greater visibility. Through the years, I've worked hard at consistently creating this content. Every day I work to follow new people in my target market. After several days if they do not follow me back, then I unfollow them. I use some automated tools in this process so it does not consume a huge amount of time but I do spend consistent time on this process. The growth of my audience on Twitter did not happen naturally or organically without any effort. It's another reality of publishing: **you have to consistently work at building your audience or platform**.

Editors and agents want to work with people who have connections to their audience (platform). Recently I spoke with an author who had worked hard on writing a manuscript. I quizzed him about his platform. Did he have a degree in this topic? No. Did he have any connections to the audience through something online or in person? No he was just an ordinary person with no online presence.

One of the ways to get an editor or agent interested in your project is to build a personal connection. Editors and agents work with people that they know, like and trust so these personal connections are a way to find the right place for your book to be published. I listed some conferences in his state and encouraged this writer to attend. Again, I encountered resistance about the cost, time and his lack of ability. I was attempting to help this author find the right connection and even build a platform. When my three or four attempts to guide him were each met with resistance and negative comments, I finally gave up and wished him well with the project. While I did not verbalize it to him, from my years in publishing, I knew it would be a long road for this author to be published (if at all).

You may not like or understand Twitter so it would not be a good place for you to build your platform. Pick one or two other online places that draw your attention and are enjoyable to use. You want them to be fun because you will be spending a lot of time on these places. Whatever sites you choose, begin right away. Internet marketing guru Seth Godin says "It is never too early to begin marketing."

Throughout my over 25+ years in publishing, I've learned one simple truth. Traditional publishers make powerful books. They have great distribution and attractive covers. Ready for the simple truth? Most of them are lacking in the ability to help their authors sell books. Authors can't delegate that responsibility to their publishers. Whether you write fiction or nonfiction, you still need to be building your platform. Fiction is based on a great story and nonfiction is based on a great idea, careful research and storytelling. Both types of writing need to have excellent storytelling—but my contention is that every author will be better positioned to actually reach customers and sell books if they have built an audience or platform which is hungry for their work.

Blogging is another powerful tool to build a platform or connection to your audience. I have been blogging since December 2004 (www.thewritinglife.ws). From this experience, I want to give you several cautions regarding blogging. First, know the audience you want to reach. Too many blogs are unfocused and have no target audience. Without this target, the blog reaches no one. The word blog comes from web log and implies the writing is spontaneous and without forethought. While you may crank out your blog without much thought, before you post it, I would encourage you to polish your writing, add an image to it and make sure every word is spelled correctly. Why do you need to make this type of effort on your blog? The digital landscape called the Internet is littered with half-baked and abandoned blogs. Whatever you write and post on a blog is around online and searchable forever. As a long-term blogger I have people who comment on articles I wrote years ago. These comments show me that even these old articles are read and show up in search engines.

Second, as you set up a blog, make sure you create a plan for posting that you can maintain and do consistently. Some people try to write three times a week and after several months find such a schedule too demanding. Like any type of regular writing project, a blog is a marathon more than a sprint. For example, I decided years ago that I could handle one blog post a week. I've written an article a week for years. The consistency is important to help you build your audience and readers.

Finally, with your blog, your task as a writer is more than simply posting on a regular basis. You also need to use every tool at your fingertips to market and promote your blog. No one will know about your new articles if you don't promote them. People can receive my blog via email and you want to include such a feature on your blog. Also, each time a new article is created, I promote these articles through my social media connections like Twitter, Facebook and LinkedIn. To market your blog articles, I encourage you to learn to use ClickToTweet. This free tool encourages readers to click the link you have created and tell others about your article. It is a simple yet effective way to market your blog entries.

Video through YouTube or Facebook Live is another platform building method. Dr. Sherrie Campbell, author of *Success Equations* (Morgan James Publishing), and I met through Twitter. A psychologist, Sherrie often speaks about toxic relationships and each week will post a Facebook video. These short videos are viewed and shared thousands of times. The videos are just one of the pieces of Dr. Campbell's platform and another example of something you could explore for your platform.

There are dozens of ways to build your platform and I've only given you a few possibilities. For further ideas, download my free 43 page Ebook called *Platform Building Ideas for Every Author* at: http://terrylinks.com/pb

A platform is important to every author. Why? Because even if you publish with a traditional publisher, it will be 80% up to every author to sell the books. Publishers will work with authors who have small or growing platforms yet *every* publisher is actively looking for people connected to their readers.

Let me ask a more basic question: who is your audience? If you say everyone, then agents, editors and other publishing professionals are going to roll their eyes. No book is for everyone. Picture your audience as a target. Which group of people is in the center of that target? Write it down. Then who is a little broader target? That audience is the next circle in the target. Do this exercise and specifically write several groups of readers for your book. For example if you have written a parenting book for parents of young children, then that is your primary audience. Teachers and leaders would be a secondary audience.

With your target audience in mind, how are you connecting with this target audience? There are multiple ways to connect with these readers: blogs, podcasts, teleseminars, radio interviews, magazine articles, and television interviews. These are only a few of the many methods.

Multiple Book Exposure & Multiple Methods Are a Key Element of Platform-Building

Book buying studies have proven that a reader has to hear about your book multiple times before they reach into their wallet and purchase a book. The number of exposures to your book is somewhere between six and twelve times before you collect a sale. A key part of your platform building process as an author is to give readers multiple exposure to your book and the availability.

For example, my biography, *Billy Graham, A Biography of America's Greatest Evangelist*, released in November 2014. I built a website: http://BillyGrahamBio.com and in the last few years, at least 50 radio broadcasters have interviewed me about Billy Graham. Each time, I attempted to save the audio recording, then I stored it on my own website (so it will not be changed or disappear). To promote my book on my platform, I've created many different social media posts. I saved these posts in a text file. With many of them, I included an audio link to one of my radio interviews. I vary the posts so it is not the same one over and over. Here's the key, even after four years from the release date, I'm posting something daily about my book with an image on social media.

As the author, I have the greatest passion for my own book. If I'm not using my platform to promote the book, then how can I expect others like my publisher to be promoting the book? The consistency of promotion with different formats and different words are a key part of how you as an author can use your platform.

Every author's platform has multiple channels and methods available to reach your audience. Are you using each of these channels with your book? Are you speaking to audiences about your book? If not, can you make some calls or send some emails to get booked and speak? Are you on a podcast or radio program talking about your book? If not, then make an effort to pitch talk show hosts and people who run podcasts to get on these broadcasts. Which social media channels are you using for your platform? Are you using these channels on a daily or regular basis to expose readers to your book? Are you varying these social media messages and stressing the benefits and giving value to the reader or listener with each one? This repeated exposure on your book using different methods is a key part of the platform building process and a necessity for every author. If you are not doing it, then take action, make a plan then execute your plan.

If you want to sell your book and encourage a buzz about it in the marketplace, be consistently working to build a larger audience. Consistent media activity on your part doesn't have to take a lot of time but the results will add up for you. Eventually you will achieve your goals if you take repeated action.

 Myth Buster Action (MBA): consistently build your platform and audience.

Chapter 4

Myth Four

Beginning Writers Have No Chance to Get Published

Some days the odds of getting published seem impossible for anyone. Literary agents and editors receive several hundred pitches for books A WEEK. The sheer volume of material makes it hard to get noticed by publishing professionals.

Some authors don't get published because they don't send in their material to be considered. It wasn't the case with an author I met last year who had a beautiful, well-written book. She had crafted her story then paid an outside editor to hone her manuscript into a riveting personal story. Week after week she sent her query and pitch to literary agents. Many times she didn't even get a response or form rejection letter. Yet she continued to send her material. Finally the manuscript landed in my in-box and I read it, enjoying the writing. I told this author about Morgan James Publishing who accepted her book and published it.

Getting your book published is the first step in the process. There are many decisions in this area such as a traditional publisher or self-publish or a hybrid publisher. Every author has to put in the work to explore these options.

Your Submission Needs to Be Electronic

Every writer should keep growing and challenging themselves to find new avenues to enter the marketplace. As an acquisitions editor at Morgan James Publishing, I know the company receives many submissions. In fact, the company receives over 5,000 submissions a year. Out of that number only 150 books are published. Yes that is a high volume of rejection but as editors, we are always looking for the right authors and compelling material.

About a month ago, I received an author contact from one of my colleagues. That day, I sent an email to this author letting her know exactly what I needed and how to submit her material. A few days ago, I got a text from my colleague asking about this author. I said she had never responded to my email. Something many people forget is email sometimes does not always reach the intended person. I reached out to this author again on email *and* picked up the phone to call her (rare for an editor or agent to call).

Later that day I began to receive her submission in hard copy on my phone—which I could not read. It was pages of a manuscript texted to my phone. I asked her to email it to me. The email came one page at a time with the hard copy attached—many emails. I went back to this author and explained I needed a single file in an electronic form as an attachment.

In conversation, I learned this author had an electronic file for her manuscript and then her computer crashed. She lost the electronic files with her computer crash. She only had a hard copy of her manuscript. With this explanation, I understood why she was trying to get me the hard copy.

I told this author how _every_ publisher requires the author to send an electronic version of their manuscript or proposal. It is the only way to get your material into the consideration process with an editor or agent. Your computer crash and the fact you don't have the file is a barrier to getting your submission considered. If you have this problem, you can do the following:

1. Retype your manuscript into a Microsoft Word file.
2. Hire a student or transcription service to type your submission into Word.

3. Forget about this book and start another one. This last point is not what I would recommend since the author has invested hours into creating her book.

I have no idea what this author is writing and whether it has any merit or not—since I did not receive it in a readable format. I've reviewed thousands of submissions during my years in publishing and never seen this particular situation. I point out several lessons from this experience:

Submit your manuscript to the editor or agent <u>in a format they can read</u>. I've met authors who do not type. If you don't type, then take a typing course or figure out your way around this barrier.

Make sure the format of your submission is not the issue. The reality is every editor and agent receives many submissions. Sometimes things do get missed and we are not perfect in this process. Just make sure it is not <u>your</u> issue before you reach out to someone else.

Follow the editor's or agent's guidelines. If you don't follow directions, then you can't get considered.

Follow-up to make sure you are giving the editor what they need. We receive volumes of material and want to help but have limitations on our own time and resources.

As a writer, you are searching for the right fit for your submission. It will take effort on your part to find this. Good communication is important every step of the way. Sometimes it takes some digging to figure out why I am not connecting with an author. I will reach out to the author and encourage them, in any way that I can, to get their manuscript to me.

No Aspect of Publishing Is Easy

In the last 10 years, the publishing world has changed. In the past, self-publishing was the poor step-sister to traditional publishing. These self-made titles often did not look professionally produced and were not accepted in libraries or bookstores. As book production has improved, more writers are trying self-publishing. These books are still not up to the writing standard of professionally published books and the average self-published title sells less than 200 copies <u>during the lifetime of the book</u>.

My preference is for authors to have the largest distribution and produce the best possible book. It's why I continue to encourage authors to create a book proposal and work with traditional publishers as well as explore other models like Morgan James Publishing (where I've worked for over six years).

While there are many ways and companies to help you create your book, at the end of the day, the key question relates to sales of the book. Is it selling? Are people buying it on a consistent basis? Are you promoting your book? One of the best ways to learn about publishing is to consistently read how-to books about writing or marketing. As you read these books and take action from the information, you will grow as a writer. I own stacks of these types of books and I make sure I read them.

Books that endure and continue to sell in the market are rare. Traditional publishers are known to be fickle in this area. I have seen this phenomenon when I've worked inside publishing houses. You work hard to get a book published and into the market, then for whatever reason it does not sell. At that point a publishing executive writes a letter to the author or literary agent and takes the book out of print. If the book sales are low, some publishers will remove the book after three to six months. It would help if publishers had a longer tolerance for the book because some books will take off after a year.

New Books Need Reviews

Several weeks ago I was skimming on Facebook and noticed one of my author friends was talking about a new book. I wrote this friend and offered to review her book. She was going to ask her publisher to send me a book. I promptly pressed on to something else and almost forgot about it. Then the review copy arrived this week. I'm eager to write a few words of review to help my friend.

I received this book from the publisher to review a short time before it launched. As a part of my process to get ready to review this book, I checked the book page on Amazon. Nine days after the launch, it looked like my review was going to be the first one. There were no reviews for this book. Reviews are important to every author because they are social proof that readers love your book. It's why I work as an author to ask others to review my book and also review books for others on Amazon and Goodreads.

I emailed my author friend about her lack of reviews. Now this author had sold thousands of copies of some of her other books. She has a full-time job—not as an author. Despite her years in publishing, I found her response interesting. Her email blamed the lack of effort on <u>the marketing department of her publisher</u>.

One of the best ways for you to take responsibility and to avoid this scenario is to create your own marketing plans. Whether you self-publish or have a traditional publisher to place your book into the bookstore, these plans are important. Whether your book launches soon or has been out for a while, you need to create and execute your own marketing plans.

A marketing plan from the author is a key element in every book proposal. The proposal is your business plan. If you have such a plan, are you taking action to execute it? Does your plan need adjustment and updating?

It Takes Author Activity to Sell Books

Before I began working inside a book publishing house, I had written more than 50 nonfiction books, ranging from children's to adult books. I have never self-published a book and always worked through traditional publishers.

However, I was unaware of the financial production numbers for nonfiction books and I found it shocking—and something critical for potential authors to understand. When I saw these production numbers, I understood that the publisher, not the author, has the largest out-of-pocket cash investment in a book.

The author never sees these figures for their books as the publisher doesn't reveal them throughout the contract negotiation process. A publisher will produce these financial calculations as simply a part of good business practices. As an author, understanding these numbers helped me see publishing as a business. Authors have huge amounts of time and emotional investment in their words.

Inside the publishing house, the editor will gather a sales projection about how many copies the sales department believes they can sell of your title the first year. That sales figure will be used to calculate the production costs of ink, paper and binding for various amounts of printing (5,000, 10,000 or 15,000 copies). As the initial print number is raised, the cost per book decreases.

You may ask, "So why not print a large volume each time?" The answer is, if the publisher prints a large number of copies, then he has to store those copies in their warehouse, plus make sure they actually sell those copies within a year. The cost of tying up financial resources to store and warehouse books that aren't selling is enormous. Also the federal government taxes publishers on each copy in storage. These tax rules have forced publishers to think long and hard about how many copies of each book to print.

Inside my former publishing house, we calculated the overall printing details of the book (paperback with general publishing look or hardcover with jacket) and the number of books to print before offering a book contract. In short, publishers pour a great deal of work into their books and financial projections before they call you and offer a book contract. Understanding this process helps you see some of the reasons it takes such a long time for an author to receive a publishing contract.

Often the publisher returns to an author with whom they have already published a book. If the publisher takes a second or third book from the same author, they are investing in that author's career and trying to build that author's audience and market. If the author's books are selling well, then the publisher will be eager for another project. Each week, publishers monitor sales numbers on their books to see if particular authors merit another book contract.

Many writers focus only on the creative aspects of writing a book and getting it published, but the executives inside a publishing house are business people who want to sell books and turn a profit. It's a delicate balance between creating the best possible product and assuring that each product has the best opportunity to sell into the market and reach the target audience.

Why You Must Understand Your Competition

Consider the competition for your book. When I have asked authors about the competition, some authors say, "I don't have any competition. My book is unique."

Another author thinks about it and says, "Everyone. My book competes with every other book."

From my years in publishing, the answer is neither one and important for every author to understand. Take a few minutes and imagine your book concept as a real book. If you have one it's easy, but if you just have an idea, think about the cover, title and your name on it. Got that image? What section of the bookstore will your book appear? With this information, think about the current titles in this section. What books are facing out on the shelf? These books are your competition. The reader could reach for your book to take to the cash register to purchase or they could reach for the bestselling title.

Next write down these titles and investigate them using tools like Google. Get any sales numbers or information about the titles. This information is important for your pitch to literary agents and editors. You also need to include these insights about your competition in your proposal. Your careful consideration here will differentiate your pitch from others—and increase the chances of a traditional publisher contracting your book.

Even if you self-publish, you need to have this ammunition for your approach to the marketplace. If your book has been in print, you still need this information about the competition. Your literary agent and editor need this information to target your book. When I worked at another publishing house, I needed this competition information before a contract could be issued.

It's an Unsolvable Mystery

Don't you love to curl up with a good mystery? It's enjoyable to turn the pages, jump in the footsteps of a detective and follow the clues. There is also some mystery in publishing that may be unsolvable. The ongoing question remains: Why do some books sell and some books fade out of print?

It happens (and has happened) to many authors—you would instantly recognize their names. Their books are out of print. As the acquisitions editor at a publisher, I had access to the list of books which had been put out of print (over a several year period). The decision to take a book out of print was made on the basis of the sales—and seemingly little else such as the author and their rise in the market. This particular list included names like Bill Myers, Luis Palau, Ross Campbell and other best-selling authors. While these particular titles had perhaps been in print for some time, the sales were not enough volume to maintain the book in print. Whether you go the traditional route or the self-publishing route on the books, it will take hard work for your books to be sold, or to continue to be in demand and in print.

An interesting book for writers to read and study is *Making the List, A Cultural History of the American Bestseller 1900–1999* by Michael Korda (Barnes & Noble Books, 2001). Korda was the editor-in-chief at Simon and Schuster and studied the bestseller lists for the last century. When you read the book, you learn the complete unpredictable nature of what makes the list and what doesn't make it.

I've heard best-selling author Bruce Wilkinson (*Prayer of Jabez*) talk about how he had decided not to write any more books at one point. He had a successful teaching and seminar ministry and had not found much success in the book area. In 1977, I heard him speak about the topic of Jabez. He had written a 200-page manuscript—and never published. Then he put together a little book about Jabez that was published. People began to talk about it. Pastors began to buy cases of the book and hand it out to their congregation. It took off. Bruce has been speaking about the *Prayer of Jabez* for many years. When the *Prayer of Jabez* was published, it was finally the right time and the right place for that particular book.

Several years ago I acquired a book from the pastor of a mega-church. The publisher worked on a promotional campaign and the author did almost 100 radio interviews when the book released. He also produced a short tract with an excerpt from the book (and the cover of the tract matched the book cover). He and members of his church handed out over 50,000 copies of this tract. Yet when he received his royalty statement with the accounting of the sales, he called me to ask about the numbers. After I investigated, I found the numbers were true. A small number of books were sold through the stores but the majority of the books had been purchased through his ministry. Something broke down somewhere in the sales process. Despite an active and successful publicity campaign, it wasn't reflected in the book sales. It is an unsolvable mystery to me.

Within a traditional publishing setting, the decision about keeping a particular book in print will boil down to the sales. There are some solid things that you as a book author contribute specifically to help this process:

❖ **Don't hold back on the author promotion of your book. Jump into it and while you are writing other things, market your book.**

❖ **Market your book even after the first initial months of the release. Some books are slow to take off and become bestsellers. I've read** *This Present Darkness* **didn't sell many copies during the first year but then through word-of-mouth marketing, the book began to take off and gained the best-seller status.**

❖ **Understand the importance of the backlist and steady sales to the publisher. I read an interesting article in** *Publisher's Weekly* **about business books. Seth Godin's** *Purple Cow* **was published by Portfolio two years earlier and at that time** had more than 150,000 copies in print after 23 printings. Or Malcolm Gladwell's *The Tipping Point* (2000 release) was on the current paperback bestseller (trade) list in *Publisher's Weekly* with over a million copies sold.

❖ Sell through multiple channels. Readers like plenty of choice when they go to purchase their books. Your book should be available in a variety of formats such as every type of Ebook, paperback, hardcover and audiobook.

Life is full of unsolvable mysteries. I've often heard this quotation about prayer: "We are to pray like it depends on us and live like it depends on God." I believe the same holds true for book marketing. We live with the uncertainty of the market but we continue to write because we know that books (and magazine articles) change lives. So we keep on even in the midst of uncertainty.

Publishing Switch and Bait

Over the last 20 years Greg Stielstra, author of *Pyromarketing*, marketed hundreds of Christian books including *The Purpose Driven Life*. During that time he noticed a disturbing trend. Some Christian authors sought fame because they believed only celebrities could influence culture. What's more, they thought to sell lots of book required hiding their Christian content. In a sort of publishing bait and switch, some authors thought they must achieve a platform with secular books—or at least books that minimized faith content before they could use their platform for good. The formula was, "First become famous and then make a difference."

Greg saw things differently. He saw authors like Lee Strobel achieve tremendous success by writing books with clear biblical content that helped people. The formula was reversed; first make a difference and then the platform will follow. "Aim at Heaven," C.S. Lewis correctly noted, "and you get Earth thrown in. Aim at Earth and you'll get neither."

And what about the myth of this chapter: beginning writers do not get published? Because it happened years ago, many people forget about a brand new fantasy writer who was looking for an agent named J. K. Rowling. There is a little discussed story about *Harry Potter* that I read originally in this article in *The Observer* (http://terrylinks. com/HarryPotter)

Almost everyone knows that J. K. Rowling was an unpublished children's writer and single mother who wrote *Harry Potter* in a coffee shop and dreamed of getting published. How was the book discovered and brought into the publishing world?

J. K. Rowling overcame incredible hurdles to secure that initial book contract. Some of those hurdles she passed through with sheer good luck. There is no other way to categorize it. Rowling's experience definitely fell outside the normal way of publishing.

Here's the two key paragraphs (in my view) from this article: "The agency, run in 'cramped' and 'near-Dickensian' offices in Fulham, south-west London, was cash-strapped until touched by Potter's magic wand. Literary folklore has it that Rowling, then a penniless 29-year-old single mother, walked into a public library in Edinburgh, looked up a list of literary agents and settled on the name Christopher Little because it sounded like a character from a children's book."

"Bryony Evens, the office manager at the time, has said that it went straight into the reject basket because 'Christopher felt that children's books did not make money'. But its unusual black binding caught her eye, prompting her to read the synopsis and show it to Little. He recalled: 'I wrote back to JK Rowling within four days of receiving the manuscript. I thought there was something really special there, although we could never have guessed what would happen to it.' He managed to sell it to Bloomsbury for £2,500, but later it reaped huge rewards from international rights and he has won a reputation as a brilliant deal-maker who puts Rowling first."

With the current exchange rates, £2,500 is just a bit over $5,000. Also this article mentions the agent has received an estimated commission of over $100 million. Not a bad return for pulling a manuscript with an unusual manuscript with black binding from the reject basket.

Don't assume your material can go into this "other" category for how it becomes published. I'd encourage you to work through the normal channels as much as possible but be aware that sometimes a project will jump to the front of the line.

Why Every Book Needs a Proposal (Even Self-Published)

No matter what method you choose in the publishing world, I encourage you to create a book proposal. Whether it is fiction or nonfiction, you need to create this document because it is your business plan for your book. Years ago as a frustrated acquisitions editor, I wrote *Book Proposals That $ell, 21 Secrets to Speed Your Success* (www.bookproposalsthatsell. com). This book has over 130 Five Star Amazon reviews and many people have used it to get published. I also have a free book proposal checklist at: www.terrylinks.com./ bookcheck and a free teleseminar about proposals at: www. askaboutproposals.com.

I've read thousands of book proposals as an acquisitions editor and a former literary agent. I continually teach on the topic because I believe many writers don't understand the critical nature of this specialized document called a *book proposal*.

On the traditional side of publishing, editors and agents read proposals. It doesn't matter whether you've written nonfiction or fiction because this document includes information which never appears in your manuscript yet is critical in the decision-making process.

Many authors have not written a book proposal because they have written a full manuscript. From my perspective of working in book publishing for over 20 years, every author should create a book proposal for their book—whether they eventually publish the book with a company where they pay to get it published, (subsidy or self-publishing) or whether they find a traditional book publisher. In the proposal creation process, the author learns critical elements about their book concept, plus they are better positioned in the marketplace.

Here are four of the many benefits of proposal creation:

1. **You Define Your Target Market.** Many authors believe their book will hit a broad target—everyone. No successful book is for everyone. Each book has a primary target audience and the proposal creation process helps you define, pinpoint and write about this audience. It is important in nonfiction but it is also important in fiction. For example, romance is the largest fiction genre yet there are many divisions within the romance genre. The proposal helps to define this division and helps the publisher understand who will be creating the sales.

   Every proposal needs a target which is defined—yet large enough to generate volume sales. You learn and achieve this balance when you create a page-turning book proposal.

2. **You Understand Your Competition. Book proposals force writers to take a hard look at what is already on the market, and what if anything they bring to the conversation.** Many new authors believe they are writing something unique with no competition. It's not true. Every book competes in the marketplace and you will be a better equipped author if you understand your competition.

3. **You Create A Personal Plan For Marketing. As you create a book proposal, you will include practical, specific and** measurable ideas that can executed when your book enters the market. The proposal will be a valuable reference tool for you because you've done this important evaluation process.

4. **You Possess A Valuable Tool To Pitch Agents and Editors at Traditional Houses.** Literary agents and editors do not read manuscripts. They read book proposals. Even novelists need a book proposal for their initial pitch to an editor or agent. And if you self-publish and are successful with selling your book, because you own everything, if you receive an attractive offer from a traditional house, then you can move the book. Without a proposal you can't properly pitch the concept and you've eliminated this possibility.

Throughout my years in publishing, I have made multiple trips to New York City and met with some of the top literary agents and editors. Almost each time, I am asked, "Where is the next *Prayer of Jabez* or *Purpose Driven Life* or *Left Behind* or _____ (name the bestselling book)?" Each of these books sold millions of copies. The *Left Behind* books continue to sell over 100,000 copies a year—and they were originally published over 20 years ago. These professionals are actively looking every day for the next bestseller. Yes they may be telling you their agency is full and they have no room on their list for your book—but the reality is something different. I encourage you to keep looking for the right fit for your manuscript. It's part of the editorial search that every writer undergoes to discover the right place for their book to be published.

 Myth Buster Action (MBA): Create a book proposal and use my book proposal checklist to guide you: http://terrylinks.com/bookcheck If you make the effort to create an excellent book proposal, then you will be ready to pitch your book at any time and any place. Also I have a free list of over 400 literary agents with their contact information at: www.terrylinks. com/agents.

Chapter 5

Myth Five

I Can't Call Myself a
Writer Unless I Publish a Book

We prize and value our books. They are permanent and have our names on the spine of the book and the front and back cover. Yet it is a myth that you are not a writer if you don't publish a book.

You will reach many more people with a magazine article than a book. The average traditional book sells 1,000 copies during the lifetime of the book. The average self-published book sells less than 200 copies during the lifetime of the book. I've written more than 60 books and understand the effort it takes to craft 50,000 or 70,000 words into a well-written manuscript. It is not something accomplished in an evening but takes time and energy. But the potential readership can be a small audience.

If you've written a Christian book, then you need to get a copy of *Your Guide to Marketing Books in the Christian Marketplace* by Sarah Bolme. This book is packed with a wide range of information and resources. Whether you are launching a new book, selling a book which has been in the market for a while or targeting special markets like homeschool, Spanish or African American, every author will find many insights in these pages.

As someone who has been in the Christian market for many years as an author and editor, I appreciated the honest and forthright information in this book. Here's some details Bolme mentions in her introduction:

- Almost half of the books published today are self-published
- The average self-published book sells between 40 and 200 copies.
- These poor sales are often because the author doesn't know how to effectively market.

Bolme writes, "When promoting the Kingdom of God, getting books into people's hands is God's business. All you can do is what you know to do. Do that and ask God to bless your feeble efforts. After all, if he can feed over 5,000 people with two small fish and five little loaves of bread, He can multiply your marketing efforts to reach thousands of people, if that is His desire. Marketing and selling books is not a sprint; it is a marathon. Too many authors give up too quickly when they do not see immediate results."

Publishing in magazines is an under-used route for authors to reach readers. As a former magazine editor, I understand the power of reaching the audience. If you want to publish books, I want to encourage you to take a different course of action. As an editor, I read many other publications and I looked for writers who could also write for me. If I write an article, it reaches many more people than my books. On the average a book may sell 5,000 copies. Certainly some books turn into bestsellers but with more than 50,000 new books a year—many books are fortunate to sell 5,000 copies.

With one article, I have reached millions of people. For a period, I was Associate Editor of a publication which reached 1.8 million people each month. The greatest feedback that I've received has been for my magazine writing. I've written for more than 50 publications over the last 30 years. When you write for periodicals, it builds your reputation as a writer with the editors. Also through magazine writing, you increase your confidence to write for publication and your ability to meet target length and deadlines. There are many benefits when you write for magazines.

How to Increase Your Publications Odds

The bulk of my magazine writing is done on assignment. How do you get an assignment? You can get an assignment when you write a query letter which is targeted to a particular audience and publication.

Which magazines do you read on a consistent basis? Your familiarity with these publications and the types of articles that they publish, gives you some needed background. Pull out the magazines that come into your home. Now organize them with several months from the same publication. Then study the contents. What types of articles do they publish? How-to articles? Personal Experience? For example, at *Decision,* where I used to be an editor, almost every article was a first-person, personal experience story. If you sent them a how-to article which is not written in the first person, you were asking for rejection. Or if you write a story about someone else in the third-person, you are inviting rejection. You learn this type of information from a careful study of the publication.

After you have studied the publications, write the publication for their writers' guidelines. Almost every magazine has guidelines for their authors. You can also use Google and often find these guidelines online. Write a simple letter asking for guidelines and enclose a self-addressed, stamped envelope for the response. You can find the address for the publication usually on the masthead of the magazine under editorial offices. Or use *The Christian*

Writers Market Guide by Steve Laube. This guide is a critical tool if you are going to write for the Christian marketplace. After reading through the guidelines, you will have some additional information. Does the publication accept query letters or prefer full manuscripts? Some magazines have a query only system. This means that you have to write a query letter (one page) and get a letter of request from the editor, before sending the full manuscript. Other publications like *Decision* do not look at query letters but only completed manuscripts.

What's a query letter? Entire books have been written on this topic and one of the best is *Irresistible Query Letters* by Lisa Collier Cool (Writer's Digest Books). A query is a single-page letter which sells your story idea. It has a four paragraph formula. The first paragraph is a creative beginning for your article. You don't write the entire article—only the first paragraph which captures the reader's interest. The purpose of this first paragraph is simply to capture the editor's attention. Editors are involved in a multitude of tasks. Reading query letters is often done at the end of the day, late at night or in a car pool on the way home. It *must* be interesting.

The second paragraph of a query includes the main points of how you will approach the article. The third paragraph gives your personal qualifications for this topic and your writing credits (if any). It basically answers the question regarding your expertise which provides the basis for the article.

The final paragraph outlines timelines and deadlines. When could you deliver the article? Make sure you give yourself enough writing time. For example, your query could say you will deliver the completed article "three weeks from assignment"). In addition, enclose a self-addressed, stamped envelope and mention you look forward to their reply. When I send my pitch, I often send it to as many as ten different publications at the same time.

Within the magazine business, there is an on-going discussion about simultaneous submissions (where you send the same finished article to several publications). If you submit the same work to many different publications at the same time, you may end up on the black list of authors. Each publication has a list of people that are blackballed. You don't want to be on that list. Also each publication has a list of authors they use regularly and call with ideas. Your goal is to get on the list of regular contributors.

A simultaneous query is not the same as a finished article. Go ahead and query several magazines at the same time on the same topic if you think you can write several different articles on the same subject. One magazine may ask for 500 words on the topic while another may approach it from an entirely different viewpoint and ask for 2,000 words. Your illustrations and information will be considerably different. If you send it to 10 magazines, you may get 10 rejections. On the other hand, perhaps you will get an acceptance or two, or at least a request to see the entire article on speculation. "On speculation" means that the editor is not under obligation to purchase your article if it doesn't meet the periodical's standards or expectations.

No one gets magazine assignments just thinking about it. As a writer, you have to take action and be regularly pitching your ideas to editors and writing query letters. Then when you get an assignment, write an excellent article and submit it on or ahead of the deadline. As you learn to write a query letter and take consistent action, you will increase your odds of publication and get published in magazines.

Writing Your Magazine Article: The Details

How do you write your magazine article? Let's explore the details in this section. As a long-time journalist writing for different publications and a former magazine editor, I'm intimately acquainted with the elements for these articles.

If you've written a query letter, then you've already written the opening for your article. Otherwise, the first step in the writing is to create a motivating opening story. The key phrase is to make it *motivating*. The opening has to propel the reader into the rest of the article so they can't stop reading.

Here's one example from my own personal story: "I've gone to church most of my life but I lived off my parent's faith until half way through my sophomore year in college." How is that? Would it propel you to keep reading? Probably not.

Here's the way my story began in a published article, "I slapped the snooze alarm for the third time and finally opened my eyes at Chi Phi, my fraternity house. Last night had been a late one. After covering an evening speech and interview for the school paper, I worked frantically on the story until just before midnight, when I dropped it into the hands of a waiting editor."

Compare these two examples. Notice the detail in the second version. I am not telling you about the experience, I am showing you. Repeatedly the writing books and teachers say, "Show don't tell." Writing coaches urge writers to use dialogue and the type of detail for a story which propels readers into an experience.

After writing the article's opening, how do you continue? If you've done your research for the article, you will not write 2,000 words for a publication that only takes 500 word articles. Because you have a target length for your article, this word count helps give definition for your plan.

Also if you've learned what the publication will use, you've created a focus. Can you summarize the point of the article into a single sentence? Complete the sentence: My article is about _____. After you've written this sentence, never wander away from this goal. Sometimes in articles I saw at *Decision*, the author would begin well then wander around and finally conclude. The articles lacked focus and the sentence statement will help you keep the article on track.

I write from an outline for each magazine piece. Normally my article will have a number of points or illustrations. A standard outline would be:

- the problem
- the possible solution
- your solution

If you're writing about a person, your outline might include different aspects of the person's life such as childhood, life before Christ and life after Christ. Write out the different points for your outline. When I write a short story, I use the same approach. What is the beginning, middle and ending? An outline keeps the writer focused on the article's goal.

Also be realistic with yourself and your writing life. Can you only write for 30 minutes a day or maybe it is only 10 minutes? Are you motivated to write the entire article in one session? Or maybe you decided to write one point from your outline during each session. Whatever your writing goal, the point is to write consistently and keep moving the article toward completion.

After you've written the article, put it away for a period of time. If you are on a tight deadline, that might involve eating lunch and then returning to continue further editing. If you have the time, you might wait several days or a week. When you return to your article read it out loud. The ear is less forgiving than the eye. Reading it out loud will point out areas for you to revise and rewrite.

The focus of your entire article will be that single sentence and keep your article in a tightly written story. It is just what the reader (and editor) needs.

Can I Write for _____ Magazine?

I love print magazines and I subscribe to a number of them. When they arrive, I frequently read them cover to cover. While I enjoy many different types of publications, as a writer, I also take a deeper look to see if there is an opportunity for me to write for the magazine.

I want to give you some of the benchmarks and resources you can use to evaluate your magazines and see if you have an opportunity to publish with them. Every editor begins the issue with blank pages to fill. These empty pages spell opportunities for freelance writers.

First, look at how long the publication has been in business. If the magazine is a new publication, the contributors have not yet been established. If the magazine has been around for years, notice who writes the articles. Are their names listed on the masthead as "contributing writers?" If so, then the magazine may be mostly staff written and does not use much freelance material.

Next use Google to search for the magazine online. Does the publication have writer's guidelines or information about submissions? If so, then they are normally open to freelance articles. Read these guidelines and follow the instructions. Does their website list themes for forthcoming issues or have a "themes list?" If you pitch an idea related to these themes, then you will get more interest from the editor because you are sending something that is in alignment with what the editor needs or has requested.

Go to your local library and use the latest *Writer's Market Guide*. Use the index to look up the entry for the magazine. What percentage of their magazine is freelance? The higher the percentage the more likely there is opportunity for the writer. Do they pay on acceptance or publication? As a writer, I prefer publications that pay on acceptance. Magazines that pay on publication may hold your article for many months before publishing (and paying).

As in book publishing, the magazine world is constantly changing. For example, I noticed recently *Architectural Digest* has a new editor. I learned this fact because each month the editor writes a brief column in the front of the magazine. Change can spell opportunity for the writer because a new editor may be open to new ideas and new pitches for the publication. To gain an assignment, you have to be on their radar. As a freelance writer, you get on their radar through professional pitching—and not just once or twice but over and over.

Every magazine is looking for dependable, professional writers who can deliver excellent writing on the editor's deadline. You will have to prove yourself but as you deliver quality writing repeatedly, then you will gain the editor's trust and become someone who is a part of their team of regular writers. The procedure is a process and begins with studying the publication then pitching appropriate articles.

Opportunity is everywhere. Use these tips to begin writing for publication.

How to Write What the Editor Wants

When you boil it down to the basics, writers and editors are both seeking the same thing: excellent writing. I've been writing for magazines for many years and I'm a former magazine editor. One of the publications (*Decision*) where I was Associate Editor reached 1.8 million people with each issue. While editors and writers are focused on excellent writing, I also understand what qualifies as "excellent" is subjective.

In this section, I want to propose three ways to improve your article or query submissions so you can improve your rate of publication success. One of the keys is to understand the role of the editor and how to write what the editor wants. The editor knows their reader and target market.

Read the magazine cover to cover with analysis before submitting. It may sound like a basic but you would be surprised at what writers pitch without ever reading the publication. As you read the magazine, study the details. Do staff members write most of the publication? Do they publish freelance writers who are not on the staff? Do they have regular features? Who writes these features and is there opportunity for you to write this material? You can learn a great deal as you study the publication. Find the publication and study the details.

Target magazines which publish their upcoming themes. Many publications, such as denominational magazines, will plan their themes for an entire year. If you pitch or write an article on the editor's list, you will get a closer look and consideration than someone who sends a random idea. Also know that seasonal and holiday pitches or articles are always needed. Think about the forthcoming holidays such as Valentine's Day, Easter, Memorial Day, Fourth of July, Thanksgiving or Christmas. Make sure you pitch at least six to eight weeks before the holiday to get consideration or your article may be accepted but not published until the next year.

Read the magazine guidelines before sending your query or article. Many publications share their guidelines online but if not, take time to write for the guidelines and review them before you write the editor.

Every editor is actively looking for great writing to fill their publication. If you follow all or several of these tips, you will improve your opportunity to touch their readers and get published.

Everyone Can Write a Personal Experience Article

Life brings each of us strange personal experiences. A recent spring I traveled to visit my mother in Kentucky. When I checked into the airport, my suitcase had four wheels. To my surprise, when I picked up my suitcase, it only had three wheels. In transit, the airline had broken my suitcase. During this trip I learned to immediately file a form with the airline and they repaired my suitcase. My personal experience can be combined with lessons and insights for the reader to create a straight-forward personal experience magazine article.

What is the difference between a regular person who has "different" personal experiences and a published magazine writer? Some people save their experience or story for small talk at their next party. A published magazine writer will make some notes about the details, the feelings, the sights and sounds plus maybe pieces of real dialogue for the story. These raw notes become the key points to write a personal experience magazine article. Almost every magazine publishes personal experience articles. In fact, the *Christian Writers Market Guide* lists over 50 publications where you can submit your personal experience article.

Here's several key action points in this process:

1. **Begin with a simple outline.** Do you have an interesting title and an engaging opening paragraph? Every personal experience story needs a logical beginning, middle and ending. You can't tell everything so use your outline to narrow the key points for your article.

2. **Make sure the end of your article has a single point** which is called a takeaway for the reader. As a former magazine editor, I've seen many submissions which fail to have a single point to their article. This is often a key reason for rejection.

3. **Review the submission guidelines** for each publication before you fire off your submission. Maybe the editor prefers a query letter. If so, learn how to write one. Or does the publication prefer the full article? Do they take simultaneous submissions? Do they take reprints? A reprint is where your article has already been published yet you retain the rights to reprint or republish it in another publication. Do they pay on publication or acceptance? Answers to these questions will help you form a list of possible publications and a game plan to submit your article.

As writers, we need to take action with our personal experiences, write them down and craft them into magazine articles. As you submit these articles, it will increase your visibility in the market and you will have the opportunity to help others through your writing.

Write an Evergreen Magazine Article

What if you could write a magazine article which could be published year after year in different publications? These types of articles are called evergreen because they can be used over and over. To write such an article takes a bit of planning on the front end of the process.

Years ago I was actively listening to recordings of the Bible. If you listen to the Bible 20 minutes a day, you can hear the entire Bible from Genesis to Revelation in four months. There are numerous audio versions of the Bible with various styles. Some versions include different voices for each character while others use the same reader for the entire Bible. Reading through the Bible is a common goal for many Christians. This topic on how to listen through the Bible can be an evergreen magazine article. There are several points you need to consider in writing an evergreen article:

1. **Rights:** What rights are you selling to the publication? An evergreen article is something you want to publish repeatedly. Some magazines will acquire all rights when they purchase an article. For an evergreen article, you want to avoid these publications—or negotiate with them for "First

Rights." When they purchase first rights, after the article is published, then the rights return to you. Ultimately for an evergreen article, you want to have "reprint rights" where you can recycle the same article in many different publications.

2. **Format and Contents:** Your article can include personal stories and how-to information yet as you write it, the contents need to be timeless or something that will work year after year. For example, an article about how to make a new Christmas tradition can be specific yet this how-to information can be easily recycled.

3. **Publications:** The world of print publications is constantly changing with new magazines starting and long-lasting ones disappearing. I recommend you get the latest version of the *Christian Writers Market Guide*. Use the current version because it will contain the most up to date publishing information. Use this reference book to find appropriate publications for your reprints.

4. **Publications Log:** Keep a simple publications log with a page for the particular article, the date you sent it to the publication and the response from the editor.

My article called *Listening Through the Bible* has been reprinted in many different publications and I expect I can reprint it again for years in the future. With some careful planning as you write, you can create an unlimited supply of evergreen articles which you are getting out into the market—and continuing to earn from it—as well as have the exposure and publication experience.

Are You Using a Magazine's Theme List?

Recently I attended a Christian writers' conference. It's one of the key places where you can build relationships with editors and learn how to meet the needs of editors. If you write what an editor needs, then you are much more likely to get published than randomly writing something and sending it into the publication. If a writers' conference is not in your plans, make plans to get to one soon. As editors, we publish people that we know, like and trust and you can build these relationships at a conference.

During an editor's panel at this conference, I heard an editor's cry for help. I'm not going to give the specific magazine but use this incident as a way to help you be more successful and on target with your magazine submissions.

This magazine editor leads a 200,000 circulation Christian publication which publishes a theme list with their guidelines. With each monthly magazine, they publish articles outside of their theme but in particular they need articles tied to their theme. In front of the entire conference, this editor mentioned several of his projected themes did not have a single article ready for publication.

As I listened to this editor's cry for help, I recalled my work at *Decision*, the publication of the Billy Graham Evangelistic Association. As associate editor, I was looking for theme related articles. For example, I needed articles about love for a February magazine (Valentine's Day). It was not easy to get these articles even for a large circulation magazine like *Decision* whose circulation at that time was 1.8 million. To gather these needed theme-related articles, I would call or email some of my author friends and ask them for submissions.

If you want to be published in magazines, in general there are two options. You can write whatever you want (inspiration) and then try to find a publication for it. Or you can look at the themes an editor has created for their magazine (their needs) and write an article to meet those needs. The second approach of writing for a particular theme is more likely to be published from my experience.

The *Christian Writers Market Guide* includes over 150 magazine listings. Many of these listings include the location of their guidelines and theme list. Another way to find these publications is to use Google with the search words "Christian editorial theme lists." I instantly found several pages of Christian publications with their theme lists.

As you meet needs of the editor (their theme list) you will be published in magazines and become a dependable resource for your editor. Don't overlook this important resource for your magazine articles.

Escape the Catch-22 of Publishing

For many years, I've known about the Catch-22 of publishing. The *Merriam-Webster dictionary* defines Catch-22 as "a problematic situation for which the only solution is denied by a circumstance inherent in the problem or by a rule." Last year in Spokane, I taught a workshop *12 Ways to Jumpstart Your Publishing Dreams* and the details are in my *Jumpstart Your Publishing Dreams* book.

Here's the problematic situation for every new writer: they want to get published yet professionals (editors and literary agents) are looking for people with publishing experience. It's the same sort of situation you face when you enter the job market and need to create a resume which lists your job experience (yet you have nothing to list). What is the best way for writers to gain publishing experience? It is not in book publishing. Books are lengthy writing projects and sometimes reach a limited number of readers (yes even when traditionally published). **The easiest way for a writer to escape the Catch-22 of Publishing is to write magazine articles.**

I have written an Ebook called *How to Succeed As An Article Writer* (www.writeamagazinearticle.com) I began my writing career in the magazine area and continue to often write for magazines. For seven years, I wrote a column for *Southern Writer Magazine* about book proposals called Book Proposal Boot Camp.

Here's another resource to help you succeed in the magazine writing world. My long-term friend, Linda Gilden, has published *Articles, Articles, Articles!* Subtitled, *A Comprehensive Guide.* This book is an excellent resource and Gilden has done a great service to the writing community publishing this book. In the introduction, Gilden tells how as a stay-at-home mom with small children, writing articles seemed her best option to get published, "My children were small and still required a lot of hands-on attention. So, my writing sessions were short, very short or nonexistent. Much of what I wrote took place in my head until naptime, then I wrote furiously hoping the children were exhausted and would sleep a long time." (Page 11)

This book contains a cornucopia of information for every writer. Here's some of the topics covered: where to get started, how to break in, types of articles, elements of articles, the rights to sell, marketing your articles and even how articles are a great way to market books and build an author's presence in the marketplace (commonly called a platform).

In addition to Gilden's own depth of experience writing for magazines, throughout the book, she includes tips from other editors, authors and professionals called "Expert Word." Also key phrases are scattered throughout the book to remind reader of key lessons such as, "A kill fee is a fee that is paid when a contracted article is never published." Whether you are brand new to the writing world or an experienced professional, you will gain insights and ideas and action steps from *Articles, Articles, Articles!*

Writers do much more than publish books. If you write for magazines and have never published a book, call yourself a writer.

 Myth Buster Action (MBA): Make a list of several magazines and articles that you want to write. Then plan to write some query letters or the entire article and get them out into the marketplace.

Chapter 6

Myth Six

The Editor Will
Fix All My Mistakes

Several years ago I met a writer who had written a romance manuscript. I asked this author, "Do you read romance?" He instantly said, "No. I just write romance." I understood his reason for writing since romance it the largest fiction genre. But if you are going to write in the genre, you should also be reading romance novels to understand the competition and to also understand the genre.

I regularly meet writers who are looking for a literary agent. Agents are looking for material to sell to publishers.

There are many agencies and they work on commission (normally 15%). If they don't sell your work, they do not get paid. Former editors make great agents because they recognize quality work—yet their focus is on selling—not spending their time fixing up writing. Your writing has to be very close to perfect for the agent to pick up their pencil and make a few improvements. Otherwise because of the volume, they simply reject it and move on to the next submission.

Bottom-line of this chapter is writing is a business. Your writing has to make money for the agent and the editor for someone to be interested in publishing your book.

One of the ways we can grow as a writer in the knowledge of our craft is to read how-to books. Even though I have an undergraduate degree in journalism and have shelves of how-to write books, I continue to read books on the craft of writing. For years I've read at least one of these types of books every month. New how-to books continue to be created and published—and I learn something from each of them.

In fact, I'm on the lookout for notices about new how-to books and I enjoy reading them and writing reviews about the books. From my experience I know other readers are making buying decisions all the time based on these reviews. I know they are important to the author. Most authors are easy to find on their website with contact information

As a way to support other writers, I encourage you to take similar action. Reach out to these writers and offer to read their book if they will send you a review copy. Yes you get a book but this book comes with some responsibility: that you read the book and write your review.

Is Writing Easy?

Within the writing community, I've often read, "There is nothing to writing. All you do is sit down at a typewriter and bleed." According to Ryan Holiday in his book, *The Perennial Seller*, this statement is attributed to Ernest Hemingway. Then Holiday continues saying, "This is a wonderful, seductive line as we consider sitting down at our proverbial typewriters. The problem is that it is preposterous and *untrue*. It is directly contradicted by Hemingway's own meticulously edited, often handwritten manuscript pages. The John F. Kennedy Presidential Library has some forty-seven alternative endings for Hemingway's *A Farewell to Arms*. He rewrote the first part of the book, by his own count, more than *fifty* times. He wrote all of them, trying them like pieces of a puzzle until one finally fit." (Page 37-38—and the italic emphasis is from Holiday)

From my study of writing, this aspect of the writing life is rarely discussed: there is hard work involved to practice the craft of storytelling and write something which sells well and continues selling year after year. The successful writers continue to learn and grow in their craft—and also grow their audience or tribe or platform. You can pick your term because different people interchange these terms. The work of writing is way more than bleeding on the page.

As a writer, I encourage you to continue to grow in your craft and your skills. You need to be practicing your writing craft with continuing to work on longer work like books but also writing shorter articles for magazines and blogs and other places. I've been publishing for many years but I continue to read a book about writing every month—and grow from reading those books.

In addition to studying about writing, I continue to try new programs and learn new skills. As I look at the various types of media that I have online, I have one area which is lacking—video. I do not have a YouTube channel nor have I recorded many videos.

Recently I've joined the faculty of the Serious Writer Academy. As a part of this faculty, I learned to record on video one of my writing workshops: *How to Create a Proposal That Publishers Want to Buy* (www.seriouswriteracademy. com/terry-whalin). Over the years, I've taught this workshop at numerous writers' conferences—but it has never been recorded on video—until now. Just use the link in this paragraph and you can learn about the video and the cost details about accessing and taking this workshop.

With my work as an acquisitions editor for Morgan James Publishing, I'm working with authors to get them a book contract all the time. Sometimes people will ask what

I'm looking for. My answer is always "good stuff." We publish many different types of books at Morgan James. I understand "good stuff" is subjective, but I also know that I recognize quality work when I see it. When you are ready to pitch your book, reach out to me and let me know how I can help you. My work contact information is on the bottom of the second page of this link: (http://terrylinks.com/MJPOneSheet)

How to Stand Out to Editors

Many writers are trying to get the attention of editors. How do you stand out as a writer in a positive way? I've seen many writers stand out in a negative way. They are memorable, but not someone that an agent or editor wants to help get published.

Here's three simple ways to make a positive impression:

1. **Deliver Good Writing.** While many writers believe they have sent an interesting and targeted submission, I've often seen poorly crafted stories and with not enough energy put into the concept. Good writing will always stand out and a fascinating story captures positive attention and earns a quick response from the editor or agent. Practice your craft in the print magazine world. If you are writing nonfiction, then learn to craft good personal experience stories. If you are writing fiction, then learn the skill of short stories—and get them

published. The experience will be valuable and help you stand out in the submission process.

2. **Submit Assigned Writing on Deadline or Early.** The majority of writers are late with their assignments. If you pay attention to the deadline and deliver excellent writing on time or early, you will stand out because such attention to detail is unusual. It will make a big difference in the impression you make with these professionals.

3. **Express Gratitude.** Whenever anyone does anything, large or small, make sure you express appreciation. We live in a thankless world where few people write handwritten notes. I make a point to continue to send handwritten thank you notes. My handwriting isn't beautiful but when I send notes, they make a positive impression. Also, when I receive thank you notes after a conference or other occasions, it is appreciated.

Working in the publishing community is all about building and maintaining relationships. Whether you are trying to sell your writing to a magazine or sell a book project to a publisher, you need to be continually aware that every time you connect with the editor or agent, you are making an impression. Make sure you stand out in a positive way.

Get the Wisdom and Experienced Insights Throughout This Book

Jane Friedman is an experienced editor and writer and a keen observer of the business aspects of publishing. She has seen firsthand what is working and what is not. With *The Business of Being a Writer*, Friedman pours her insights into the pages of this well-crafted book.

Many writers ignore the business aspects of publishing—to their own detriment. As Friedman writes in the introduction: "Here's the biggest danger, if there is one: Business concerns can distract from getting actual writing done and can even become a pleasurable means of avoiding the work altogether. No one avoids writing like writers. Producing the best work possible is hard and focusing on agents, social media marketing or conference-going feels easier. Writers may trick themselves into thinking that by developing their business acumen they improve as writers—but all the business acumen in the world can't make up for inferior writing." (Page 10-11)

The Business of Being a Writer is packed with insights. I highly recommend you get this book, read it—but more importantly apply the information to your writing life.

Read How-To Books

As you can tell from reading this chapter, one of my favorite ways to learn about the writing craft and market is through reading how-to books. I have purchased shelves of these books over the years—and they are not just for appearance. I know some people buy books and do not read them. On a consistent basis, I read these books, mark in them and take action from the suggestions inside the pages. Another one of these books that I recommend would be *Just Write* by James Scott Bell. I've known Bell for many years, admired his work and his commitment to the craft of writing. I do not write fiction but have spent most of my writing life in the nonfiction world (yet I acquire fiction and read fiction).

Whether you write fiction or nonfiction, you need *Just Write* to learn from this skilled teacher and bestselling novelist. Every chapter of this book is packed with insights. I encourage you to read with a yellow highlighter. The book is broken into two sections: Unforgettable Fiction and A Rewarding Writing Life. Each section has four chapters. Whether you have written numerous novels or never written a novel, you will profit from Bell's instruction.

Writers cannot depend on their editor or literary agent to fix their mistakes. If you believe this statement, it is a myth. Editors and agents have large volumes of submission material coming their direction. They have limited time to read any of this material. If it isn't perfect, then they reject it. In some rare cases, if the material is 80% to 90% finished, the editor or agent will not reject it but put it into the consideration process. If your work isn't ready to show to an editor or a literary agent, I encourage you to hire a freelance editor so your work is in the best possible shape before it goes to the professional.

 Myth Buster Action (MBA): Be continually learning and make a commitment to regularly study how-to books on the craft of writing. Join a critique group and grow as a writer.

Chapter 7

Myth Seven

Good Writers
Are Born Not Made

Often writers see writing in black and white terms. You are either a gifted storyteller or not. These people believe writers are born with their gift and not taught the skill of writing. This concept is another myth of publishing.

The writing world is a strange combination of skill and talent. Until you learn about what the publishing world wants and submit your material, you don't know if you have talent or not. It's true: if you don't try, it won't fly.

Many years ago as a young writer, my Indiana journalism professors taught me about manuscript submissions. For example, my magazine writing class professor, Floyd Arpan had a rule with our articles for class. If he found two errors, spelling or grammar, then we received an "F", on our assignment. Talk about frightening. The redeeming factor was the grace which Mr. Arpan built into his class. If you received an "F", you got a second chance to revise your work and turn it in a second time then he erased the first grade. He had this type of system in place before computers so we produced our ten-page magazine articles on a typewriter. If you made a mistake or error, you had to retype the entire page. This type of training for a young journalist was invaluable to me.

For about ten years after college, I left my writing and went into linguistics. When I returned to it about thirty years ago, I had to learn the system for manuscript submissions. What does it mean to have your material in manuscript format for a magazine? What in the world is a query letter and how do you write a successful one?

In this electronic age, I've learned my interaction with editors even via email is important. As my wife likes to remind me, you only get one chance to make a first impression. With an email message, it's almost too easy to fire off a missive or an email with typos and spelling errors. It's important for any writer to think about such issues with their communication— and reminder to myself as well. It makes me work hard at my email query letters or my nonfiction book proposals or any other type of writing. Your craft shows in every bit of communications.

Always Be Knocking On Doors

It takes great skill to fish successfully. While some people fish for a hobby, the seasoned fisherman knows he has to fish many times to gain skill and also to catch fish. To be honest, it has been years since I've been fishing but I "fish" every day. A fisherman puts his line into the water and is positioned to catch a fish. I put quotations around the word "fish" since I'm using fish for the word networking or connections. You have to be in the market talking and connecting with others *every day* to make a difference with your writing. Yes you need to craft an excellent book and use good storytelling. I always encourage writers to learn that skill but you need something more than good writing. You need the right connection.

Much of publishing (and any business) is a matter of making the right connection with the right person at the right time at the right place. You can't make that connection working alone in your office at your computer or curled up with your legal pad writing your story.

What steps are you taking today to "fish" or network with others? It begins with your goals for your writing. Do you want to sell more books? Do you want a traditional publishing deal or are you going to self-publish? Do you want to build your platform or group of readers? Do you want more people to know who you are and what you are doing? Then you have to make a conscious effort every day to reach out and touch other people.

Some of us reach out to others through Twitter. I follow 800 new people every day—people within my target market of publishing. It does not consume lots of time but the consistent effort is important to my constant expansion of these connections.

Also I dig into my network of friends and connections. I pick up the phone and call people leaving little messages or connecting with them for a few minutes. Yesterday I spoke with several literary agent friends. Why? Because these agents represent numerous authors who they want to get published. Those agents need to be reminded that I'm constantly looking for great authors to publish through Morgan James. Our publishing program will not be right for every one of their authors. Yet it will be perfect for some of them. I'm looking for the right author—every day.

I have authors who have submitted their manuscripts and I'm scheduling calls with them to see if Morgan James is the right fit for these authors. I spend a great deal of time on the phone and answering my email but it's part of my daily work. Your daily work will be different but are you working every day at expanding your connections? I hope so.

I think about activity in the past which has been productive for me. For example, I've made terrific connections speaking at conferences. I'd like to do more speaking next year. It will not happen if I don't take any action. Instead,

I'm making a list of conferences where I'd like to speak and conscious of who runs these conferences. Can I fill a need for this event with a workshop or keynote? There are numerous conferences and events where I can help others—but I have to be proactive to get on their radar.

I'm eager to continue to promote my *Billy Graham* and *Jumpstart Your Publishing Dreams* books (as well as other books that I've written or been involved with). Can I book a radio show or podcast or do a guest blog post or some other event to get in front of a new audience? The answer is yes but from my experience it does not happen without my initiative (sometimes but rarely). Most of the time, these opportunities come through proactive pitching and follow-up work. Are you building this type of fishing into your daily schedule? Throughout my day, I will be emailing and calling people. You have to have a line in the water to catch fish. What steps are you taking?

A Word about Rejection of Your Queries and Manuscripts

An article or query may be rejected for many different reasons. Maybe the publication has already purchased an article on that topic. Maybe they've recently assigned it to another author. Maybe they have an article on that topic coming in an issue which is already in production but not printed. There are many different reasons for rejection which are outside of your control as a writer.

Sometimes even a rejection brings an assignment. Several years ago, I had queried a number of magazines about writing on listening to the Bible on tape. I targeted the January issues of publications for this short how-to article. Every magazine rejected it.

Several weeks later, I received a phone call from a new editor at *Christian Life* magazine. They too had rejected the idea. "We're sorting through some old queries," she explained. "Would you be able to write 500 words on the topic in the next three weeks?" No problem. That little article turned into one of my most popular articles for reprint in other publications.

I prefer writing on assignment and you can snag magazine assignments as you learn how to write a riveting query letter. You want the editor to read your letter and be compelled to pick up the phone and call you for more information or an assignment. Or you want that editor to open an email and write you immediately asking when you can have the article ready for their magazine. I hope you can see the importance of this skill as a writer.

Because I've been published repeatedly in different magazines, many mistakenly believe I was born this way. Wrong. In this process, I have received many rejections.

Years ago at Indiana University I took a magazine writing course. In this journalism class, we were required to write several ten-page magazine articles. My key mistake was a lack of understanding of the market or the audience for the publications. When you write your query letter, you have to focus on both of these aspects. You want the idea to be perfect for that particular publication and you want to think about the publication's audience when you write the query. If you don't handle these two basics, then I can almost guarantee rejection. My writing and my research for the college articles was right on target—yet these articles were never published because they had no market or audience in mind. Don't make that same mistake.

While the bulk of this chapter is about magazine writing, for book authors, I encourage you to read Noah Lukeman's how-to book, *First Five Pages: A Writer's Guide to Staying Out of the Rejection Pile.* To many people, it sounds cruel that in the first five pages you can determine if you want to read the rest of the manuscript. It's true. If you stood in my place, you would be able to glean a great deal of information about the author and their manuscript—and be able to determine if it's right for your publishing situation. I'm returning this submission with the standard rejection note. I have no time to critique manuscripts and it's not my role. Critique services are available for such matters. The publishing world is subjective.

I love a manuscript and another editor can't use it. It's a matter of continuing to search for a connection and someone to champion your manuscript and get it published. They are good lessons to consider about first impressions.

Myth Buster Action (MBA): Learn to write a one-page pitch letter called a query then regularly send out these queries to magazines and get a writing assignment.

Chapter 8

Myth Eight

Self-Publishing is the Best Way to Get My Book Out into the Market

Publishing a book has never been easier. Almost everyone has a keyboard and a computer with the ability to crank out words and produce a manuscript—whether nonfiction or fiction. Authors struggle to find a literary agent and a traditional publishing deal. They get tired of crafting an excellent product, the waiting, and the rejection letters. Instead they decide to self-publish because that direction looks easy.

For over 20 years, I've been reading about publishing, writing and working in this business as an editor and writer. I encourage you to read this recent article from Jane Friedman, former editor at *Writer's Digest* and publishing expert. (www.terrylinks.com/2016Publishing)

I want to include a brief section of Friedman's article:

"Back in 2012, there were many headlines about the tremendous growth in self-publishing output as demonstrated by the increase in ISBNs used by indie authors.

Since then, Bowker—the agency that issues ISBNs in the United States—has continued to release annual stats that still show growth in the sector, but these numbers always come with important caveats, including:

- **Bowker's figures don't reflect all of the self-publishing activity out there.** They can't count books that don't have ISBNs, and a considerable volume of self-pub titles are published and distributed without ISBNs.
- **Bowker's counts are for ISBNs, not book titles.** A single book title may use several ISBNs (e.g., one for the print edition, another for the Ebook edition, and so on).

According to Bowker, ISBNs for self-published titles in 2015 reached 727,125, up from 599,721 in 2014, representing a 21% increase in one year. The increase since 2010 is 375%.

But I think more important is where the growth occurred. Bowker's numbers indicate more authors are using Amazon's CreateSpace, which is free to use; older, fee-based self-publishing services are falling out of favor. Here's a selected glimpse (again, remember these are ISBN counts coming out of each service per year):

- CreateSpace titles in 2010: 35,693
- CreateSpace titles in 2015: 423,718 (+1,087%)
- Author Solutions titles in 2010: 41,304
- Author Solutions titles in 2015: 23,930 (-42%)

The only area of Author Solutions' business that saw an ISBN increase in 2015 is WestBow, the Christian self-publishing imprint marketed through Thomas Nelson. Note that Penguin Random House, which used to own Author Solutions, sold it off in January 2016, unloading what was probably seen as an albatross."

Are these statistics a surprise to you? The increase of over 1,000% percent on CreateSpace *was startling*. If you publish through CreateSpace, your book is only on Amazon and not available in other formats.

If you decide to self-publish, understand several facts: First, you are establishing a world-wide sales record of your publishing efforts. Traditional publishers and literary agents look at this information to decide if they are going to publish your next book or take you on as a client. Second, you are in complete control of your work which may feel easier but also you are responsible for all the details of the book creation (excellent cover design, well-crafted writing, distribution and sales).

Yes the creation of books has never been easier. Here's the reality that few people will tell you: **making the book is easy but getting people to purchase the book will take hard work and persistent effort.** It will be easier to make sales, if you have developed relationships with people in your target market and connected with them often. More specifically, if you connect with your audience through an email list and speak to them face-to-face, then yes, you can sell your book.

If You Are Going To Self-Publish

When I teach at a writer conference, I often meet people who have self-published their book. Some of these authors will meet with me and see if an editor or a literary agent will be willing to move their book to a traditional publisher. Such a move for an author is rare but possible. The move depends on several factors. When you have self-published (even just using CreateSpace on Amazon), you are starting to establish a public sales track record for your book. With a few keystrokes a publishing insider can find out this sales information. If it is thousands of copies, then you can likely make a move to a traditional house. If it is a few hundred copies (which is more typical), then making a change will be much harder. Recently a writer pitched a novel saying they were a published author. I checked the name of the publisher and instantly recognized it as the self-publisher, Publish America. If you want to learn a lot about this particular publisher and their reputation in the marketplace, simply go to Google and type in the words "Publish America" and in a few entries you can see a great deal of the negative public opinion about this company.

If you have a market for your book or you speak often and need to sell something in the back of the room or any number of other good reasons, self-publishing is an option. I'll be the first to tell you that I've read a great deal of poorly produced self-published books as an editor or literary agent. It is rare for self-published books to succeed. My books have been with traditional, easily-recognized publishers. Many writers will ask me about self-publishing and because I don't know all of the details about different companies, it is difficult to know where to refer them.

When someone has decided to self-publish, they often do not take the time or energy to research the reputation of a publisher or the distinctions between the various self-publishers. Here's a resource which you should consider because it provides a wealth of information and removes some of the "guess work." For the unskilled author, it is hard to sort through the self-publishing company ads and determine which one is right for them and their budget. I recommend you get a copy of *The Fine Print of Self-Publishing, third edition, The Contracts & Services of 45 Self-Publishing Companies—Analyzed, Ranked & Exposed* by Mark Levine.

In the second chapter, Levine gives the reasons to read this book: "If you decided to buy a television or a car, you might read Consumer Reports to find the best price and highest quality. Spending hard-earned money to publish your book should be approached with the same care. But, unlike buying a car, your book is an extension of you. If you choose any publisher ranked "Outstanding" or "Pretty Good" in this book, you won't get stuck with a Lemon. This book is all about helping authors find and choose a publisher that offers a superior product at a fair price." Also you should know that Mark Levine has started his own self-publishing company, Mill City Press, which is not included in the 45 companies he analyzes and ranks.

"Here are a few reasons why you need to read this book:

- To know what you need to look and watch out for when choosing a self-publishing company
- To understand what these self-publishing contracts really say and how to negotiate better terms with a publisher

- To get the most value for your money by not overpaying for services or book printing and by getting the highest royalties" (p. 8)

What's fascinating about this book is Levine's editor took the same size book specifications to each of the companies, got their contracts, then studied and compared them. As Levine writes, "This time around, my editor contacted each publishing company discussed in this book as a prospective author—just like any of you would. The difference between you and her is that I armed her with the tough questions to ask, regarding justifications for **50%–200%** printing markups, excessive publisher royalties, and more." (my bold on the percentage of markup)

Also Levine, a lawyer, provides a detailed explanation of a publishing contract and the different elements which an author should be concerned with and what to watch for in the different clauses.

This book is eye-opening and educational for any author considering self-publishing. Why is it important? I want to include another key quotation from Levine's book, "The reason I keep putting out new editions of this book is because, now that I speak to writers' groups and at writers' conferences all over the country, I always meet people who got scammed—really scammed. In May 2007, I met a nice man who had been conned out of $35,000 to publish his book. His $35,000 got him 3,000 hardcover copies of his book that he couldn't sell, a lot of debt, and a series of lies from an unscrupulous publisher. I can promise you that, if you follow the advice in this book, you won't get ripped off by any self-publishing company and that you may, in fact, negotiate a better deal. If you don't follow the advice here you may find yourself out a lot of money and involved with an unethical publisher." (p. 9)

In the early part of the book, Levine cautions that every self-published author should have their book professionally edited. It's one of the main failures in many of the self-publishing books that come across my desk. These books are often filled with simple errors which any beginning professional editor would have caught and fixed. If you wonder which companies are covered in this book, you might be as surprised as I was with some of the companies that fell into the "companies to avoid" category. To show the depth of Levine's analysis, one of the companies, BookPros, in the outstanding category, is online. This book doesn't cover every possible self-publishing company, but many of them are included. I applaud Levine for his careful analysis and research and by serving the broader writing community with *The Fine Print of Self-Publishing, Third Edition*.

POD and Self-Publish Disconnect

I'm involved in a couple of online writing groups and no matter how many times you say it, there seems to be a broad misconception about self-publishing and POD publishing

(POD means print on demand). These books simply don't appear in the bookstores.

Please don't misunderstand me. These self-published and POD books have their place in the market—particularly if you have a means to sell the books to individuals or companies. For example if you speak often and would like to have a book to sell in the back of the room, you can easily get a self-published book or POD book to use in these situations. Just don't expect to sell your book to bookstores.

Last week a well-meaning author celebrated his first printed book, which was POD. He was holding it in his hand—always exciting. He was plotting a strategy to get his book in as many bookstores as possible and asking for help from other authors in the group. If you are going down this path, it shows a clear disconnect with the realities of the market.

Here's a bit of what I told him. "Congratulations on your book release and I celebrate with you—but after more than twenty years in this business and over 60 books in print—and working as an acquisitions editor over the last five years—I am going to have to give you a bit of a reality check. You will struggle and find it almost impossible for bookstores to stock your POD or self-published book. It's one of those messages that the POD companies and self-publishing places don't tell you (they want to get your cash and get your book in their system). Yes, your book is listed on Amazon.com (easy for anyone to do—even with a POD book) but getting it into the bookstores is a completely different story. I've been telling writers for years about the ease of getting a book printed—now getting it into the bookstores and ultimately into the hands of consumers, that's a different story.

"Retailers dislike self-published books. Every retailer that I've talked with about this issue (and I've invested the time to talk with them) have countless stories about the difficulties of these books. They have re-stocking problems and problems with the quality of the products (typos, editing, etc.).

"Here's the real test for you: go to your local bookstores and ask them if they are carrying any self-published title on their shelves. Visit the big box stores like Barnes & Noble or Books A Million as well as your mom and pop smaller independent bookstores. You will be surprised with the answer. It will be unlikely you will find a single copy among any of the thousands of books."

We can't say it often enough—the bookstore market is a closed system. It primarily deals with distributors and large and small publishers. It's why we work hard to get our books into the traditional publishing marketplace. It's why you go through the effort and hard work to create an excellent book proposal or book manuscript or novel, and then sell that idea to a publisher. Then your book is available in any bookstore—and can have the possibility of sitting on those bookshelves. You can feel free to expend the effort and energy to market to bookstores and try and place your book, but from my experience and others, it will be frustrating and likely not sell many books. I believe your marketing efforts are better served in other markets (outside the bookstore)."

No matter what I write, a number of you are going to take the leap into self-publishing. Here's several action steps if you go this route:

1. **Work with an experienced editor** to create an excellent book.

2. **Work with professional cover designers** and people to format and produce a book where every detail looks like something from one of the big five traditional publishers. This means including elements like endorsements and words on the spine of the book (including a publishing logo on the bottom of that spine). Many self-published books are missing key elements which become striking signals they are self-published such as leaving off the barcode or doing this code improperly (without the price).

3. Keep working consistently to **grow your audience**. As I mentioned in the last chapter, work daily on your platform and reaching your audience. You need to try new avenues to market and sell your book.

4. **Continue to learn all you can about publishing.** Get a copy of my *Book Proposals That Sell* and study the publishing insights in this book. (www. BookProposalsThatSell.com)

5. **Never give up on your book.** As the author, you have the greatest interest and passion for your book. This statement is true no matter whether you are traditionally published or self-published. Always be looking for new opportunities to write or speak about your book.

This last point is something I try and model with my own books. For example, I continue to do radio interviews for my Billy Graham biography (www.BillyGrahamBio.com) which came out in 2014. If you go to my book site, you will see my recent interviews in the online pressroom link in the upper right hand corner. I'm actively doing these steps which I encourage you to take.

 Myth Buster Action (MBA): Study the different models of publishing and see which one is best for you. Don't presume you will self-publish.

Chapter 9

Myth Nine

My Book Will Be a
New York Times Bestseller

Every business has a pinnacle of success. It is the ultimate mark of achievement. In book publishing, this mark of success is tied to winning a particular award or getting your book on a particular bestseller list. I've heard many writers proclaim their book will be a *New York Times* bestseller. While it is an admirable goal, just making such a statement is another publishing myth because of the difficulty involved. It is equivalent to a brand new actor proclaiming he is going to win an Oscar. Eventually, this actor may win an Oscar but rarely does it happen right away.

When an author lands on the *New York Times* list, the achievement is forever carried with their publishing life. They are introduced as a *New York Times* bestselling author. In many ways, it is the holy grail of publishing to achieve such a milestone. I've never achieved such a milestone but I know a number of authors who have reached this goal. Several years ago, I moderated a panel with three members of the American Society of Journalists and Authors who have become *New York Times* bestselling authors.

As the moderator, I pulled together the speakers and organized the session into three parts: the pitch or the proposal, the writing, and the promotion and life changes that came from the experience. I asked each speaker to pull together some tips and suggestions into a handout. This event was a "members only session" for the ASJA. In other words, you have to be a member of this organization (about 1400) and have registered for the conference and traveled to New York City for the event (an even smaller number). Here's the handout for this event (www.terrylinks.com/nytwh). This document is nine pages of solid information and insight.

I encourage you as an author to continue to market your book, yet understand reaching the *New York Times* bestseller list is not easy or simple. Many people seek it but few attain it. For the majority of authors, it is a myth for them to reach any bestseller list—not just the *New York Times* bestseller list but others like the *Los Angeles Times*, *USA Today* or *Wall Street Journal*.

In this chapter, I want to focus on several practical steps every author can take to help generate additional book sales on an ongoing basis. One of the most neglected areas for authors is the book launch. From working with authors on book production, the final push to complete a book and get it ready to print can be grueling. There is a lot of detail work to finalize a book for printing and when it is finished, there is a huge relief. Yet it is not a time to stop and do nothing. This silent period is called the pre-launch stage. To become an effective book selling author, it is the time for you to crank even more energy into this pre-sales process.

Many authors let down and do nothing during this stage. The exceptions and successful authors will use this time to promote the pre-sales on the book, write press related materials, hire a publicist and gather a launch team or at least people to write reviews. I'm going to give you more details about each of these activities.

Create a Pre-Launch Campaign

The period when the book has been completely produced and finalized but not released into the bookstore is called the pre-sales season. As an author, one of the most effective actions you can take is to organize a pre-sales campaign. Dave Jarworski, was one of the early employees at Microsoft and the winner of the first Microsoft sales award from Bill Gates. He ran an effective pre-sales campaign for the launch of his book. After he left Microsoft, Dave and I worked together at Christianity.com. We kept in touch and Dave wrote a book about Microsoft called *Microsoft Secrets* (www.microsoftsecrets.com). Dave gathered unusual resources with his book such as some unpublished videos and launched a pre-sales campaign for this book. If you pre-ordered the book, and after your order, returned to Dave and told him (giving an order number for example), you got access to these extras. The pre-sales campaign drove people to pre-order the book from different bookstores. Also the pre-sales campaign is something Morgan James can promote to our bookstore sales team who in turn promoted it to the bookstores. When *Microsoft Secrets* launched, the physical books were sold into the majority of the bookstores throughout North America and Canada. Authors who do not have a pre-sales campaign will sell into a limited number of physical bookstores, but because of the pre-launch campaign, *Microsoft Secrets* received much broader distribution than normal (and increased sales as a result).

Because a successful campaign was launched for the book, this author activity spilled into other areas such as foreign rights. At this writing, *Microsoft Secrets* has been sold into two additional languages besides English, Vietnamese and Simple Chinese. Ironically after 22 years away from Microsoft, recently Dave Jaworski rejoined Microsoft as an employee. Worldwide Microsoft has over 154,000 employees. To create your own pre-sales campaign, you can study the activities of other authors and watch how they launch their books. You may need website or other help with this process. Get several recommendations before selecting the right person to help you.

Hire a Publicist

An effective publicist can be a great asset to you as an author in this pre-launch phase of publishing. Yet like hiring an editor, literary agent, or anyone else in publishing, you have to use wisdom and all your resources to find the *right* publicist. Rick Frishman, who ran one of the largest public relations firms in the United States for many years, often tells audiences these firms have a solid "guarantee": that they will charge you every month. A typical publicist fee is $3,000 to $5,000 each month. With these amounts of money, you can quickly spend a lot of resources with little results if you aren't careful.

As a cautionary story in this area, I acquired a book for Morgan James several years ago where I had a lot of hope for great success. One of the co-authors had sold their company for millions of dollars and they had a large publicity budget to launch their book. As these authors told us their plan, it had one glaring red flag: their publicity firm. We had never heard of this firm and we've worked with many different publicists over the last 15 years. This firm may have a great reputation for getting their clients on television programs. These authors produced an excellent book but they ran through $30,000 on their publicity campaign with this firm and did not sell books.

To avoid this type of disappointment, I recommend several steps to hire a publicist:

- Get a number of recommendations
- Interview each one and speak with their clients about their results
- Check their reputation online (type the name of the company + complaints)
- Check with your publisher for recommendations

Ultimately, you are making an important decision to hire a publicist and you want to make sure you get value from this expense.

Understand the Role of a Book Publicist

Whether a traditional and recognized publisher launches your book or a self-publisher, the author has to be engaged in the promotion and marketing of their book. One of the key players in this process is the book publicist. Many of these publicists have valuable connections and relationships with media and others to help you promote your book.

Recently I finished reading a new book from publicist Claire McKinney, who has worked in publicity for major publishers for over 20 years and is a recognized expert in self-publishing appearing on *The Today Show* for example. Do *You Know What A Book Publicist Does?* is the name of McKinney's book with the subtitle, "A Guide for Creating Your Own Campaigns." As the number of new books entering the market increases *every day*, authors need to understand the role of a book publicist and how to work with them in the process of book promotion. Managing expectations about what a publicist can do for a writer is great information and woven into the fiber of this book.

The promotion or sale of any book is tied to key connections and relationships—for example to the media. Book publicists like Claire McKinney have been building these relationships for years. Every author needs to understand their role in publishing. *Do You Know What A Book Publicist Does?* fills a critical role in this process with pointed insights throughout.

McKinney answers common author questions like what is a press release and what is a book launch and the best time to launch a book? The answers are packed with her years of experience in such tasks.

In the section on Reaching the Media, McKinney writes, "I've found that "fear" is the one thing that holds most people back from reaching out and from developing good pitches. Of course, you don't want to be insulting, using the words "extraordinary" or "dynamic" just to create hype doesn't help either. If you are honest about your intentions and what you are looking for, you are more likely to get a response. It takes extra effort, but that is also how you will build a relationship with the contact that could benefit another book, or could enrich your experience in another way. If you don't ask, you don't get. I'm sure you know that expression. If you get a snappy response, chalk it up to a bad day. What is the worst that can happen?" (Page 100-101)

Beyond the Radio Interview

As an author, your publicist will book you on radio programs. These radio programs are wonderful opportunities to talk about your book. The talk show host normally receives a series of interview questions ahead of time. These radio hosts interview different authors day after day on their program. You can't assume the host has read your book—and you are better off assuming they have *not* read your book. Instead they will use the interview questions to speak with you about your book.

For example, I've done about 50 radio interviews about Billy Graham and my biography. I'm asked the same questions over and over. Yet each time, I answer them with enthusiasm as though I'm hearing the question for the first time. Depending on the radio program, often these shows only cover a certain area of the United States. How do you get more mileage from these interviews?

First, ask for a recording of the interview. Sometimes the radio station will put it on their site after the interview.

Other times if you ask, they will email the audio file to you. You have to ask for it or search for it and preserve this audio file.

With this audio file in your possession, the next step is to listen to it. Is it a solid recording? Do you need to cut out local commercials or anything to make it universal and just your interview? I use an audio program called SoundForge for this editing process. Just like Microsoft Word edits words, you can use SoundForge to edit audio files.

I create or check to make sure I have a solid recording of my interview. Next I upload the audio file to my own hosting site. If I just link to the interview from someone else's site, they are in control and I've had these links disappear. When I put it on my own site, I know the interview is always going to be available online and never disappear. You have to make sure you preserve the interview on a site that you control.

The final step is to incorporate this interview into your on-going social media efforts (Twitter, Facebook and LinkedIn). Here's an example from one of my radio interviews about my Billy Graham book: http://terrylinks.com/KPOFGrahamInt The interview was recorded months ago, yet because it was a morning radio show, it sounds like it happened yesterday. The listener doesn't need to know the real date.

Because I reuse these interviews, people will regularly email me saying they heard my interview and compliment me. I respond with gratitude and never say when it actually happened (not relevant information for that listener). These recordings continue to promote and drive book sales and exposure for my book—long after the interview. Like many of these actions in the marketing area, they do not happen unless the author takes control of the interview (storing it on your website) then continue to promote it.

Gather a Group to Write Reviews

Do you have book reviews for your book? Are they "honest" reviews or something you have orchestrated from friends and family? It is hard work to write a good book and get it into the market. Whether you work with a traditional publisher or self-publish, I hope you have produced an excellent product. At some point in the process, you are ready to release this book into the market. What will others say about your writing? The natural tendency is to expect everyone to glow about your book and send you accolades.

Yet that expectation is not reality. Not every review will be five star. These reviews are important social proof from readers and feedback to you as the author. Several years ago, I met a novelist who claimed to have sold thousands of books on Amazon. Yes, this author touted amazing numbers for her book sales. Yet when I looked on Amazon, there was one review—and the author had written that review. If you don't think this result is unusual, take a few minutes and look at any bestselling novel on Amazon. If the book has been selling well, then people enjoy it and write reviews—often hundreds of reviews.

I look at other books (even self-published) which have less than five reviews—even if they have been out on the market for several years. Again this absence is social proof of the quality and feedback from readers. Your book should have reviews and as the author, you need to take responsibility to get these reviews.

As the author, you can create a launch team. Recently I've been involved in the launch of several books. I've filled out applications to be a part of the launch team. These applications ask why I should be included. The launch director creates a private Facebook area with encouragement to read the book and post reviews. Recently I got added to a launch team that said they were only going to let 500 people to be on their launch team. What a huge team but see the social proof these authors are gathering for the launch of their book?

Your team may be smaller than 500. Can you launch your book with 25 reviews on Amazon? To launch with 25 reviews, you will need to gather at least 50 people who agree to review your book and will post a review during the week your book is launched. Why so many more than the 25 you need? Even though you do your work and the person has committed, not everyone carries through with their commitment. Maybe the book doesn't reach them in the mail. Maybe they get ill. Maybe they have some family emergency. Life happens for every person and they don't carry through with their promised review. As the author, you need to recognize this fact and move beyond it with even more people to write the review.

This process of organizing and getting reviews takes work and effort from the author. Bestselling author Tim Grahl has written about this process and guided numerous bestselling authors. He has a valuable article here: http://timgrahl.com/amazon-reviews/. Be sure and scroll to the bottom of the page and get his Amazon Review Package. You give Tim Grahl your email address but get an excel spread sheet, sample emails and much more. This package can be a valuable resource for you to gather your reviews—if you use it. Also I encourage you to get this free teleseminar that I created with Dana Lynn Smith about reviews: http://yourbookreviewed.com/

In your request to the reviewer, you are asking for an "honest" review. Not every review will be a Five Star Amazon review or glowing. A while back, one of my Morgan James authors called me almost in tears asking what she should do with a one star review. My advice: do nothing. Don't comment back. Don't complain to Amazon. Do nothing. The fact that you've received a variety of reviews is good for your book. In fact, the one or two star reviews validate the four and five star reviews you have received. The low reviews show others your reviews are from real readers.

Over ten years ago as a frustrated acquisitions editor, I wrote *Book Proposals That Sell*. The book has hundreds of Five Star Amazon reviews and it has helped many people. It continues to be reviewed. About four months ago, I received a detailed One Star review. Did I read the review? Yes. Did I take any action or reach out to this reviewer? No. This book continues to help people. You need to fix what you can, then let the rest go—and continue working on getting reviews.

More Insights about Getting Book Reviews

Often I see books launch into the market with zero reviews or only a few reviews. With over 4500 new books entering the marketplace every day, it is a challenge for any author to find readers—and to find readers who will write a few sentences of honest review and post it on Amazon and Goodreads and other sites.

First, take your own responsibility for getting book reviews. Whether your book is brand new or has been out for a while, continually work at getting reviews. When you get a review—especially a positive one—promote or tout that review on your social media connections (Facebook, Twitter, LinkedIn, etc).

Second, study this 16-page article from Jim Cox, editor-in-chief at Midwest Book Review. (http://terrylinks.com/May2017JCR). I found this interview with Shelby Londyn-Heath was filled with insights. Jim has been in his position for over 40 years and provides an amazing free service to help people discover books. I want to make several points from this article:

- ❖ They receive an average of 2,000 titles a month to review and select 600 to 700 a month to actually review.
- ❖ Books are rejected for possible review for several reasons including not following their submission guidelines, poor covers and serious production problems.
- ❖ *Midwest Book Review emphasizes self-published books and books from small presses. Cox also encourages authors to produce excellent books—edited and designed well. These foundational elements are missing in many books and some of the reasons for books not to be reviewed (rejected in this process).

As I mentioned in an earlier chapter, mega-promoter P.T. Barnum said, "Without promotion, something terrible happens. Nothing." This statement is true for promotion and marketing but it is also true for almost every aspect of the publishing business. If you are not tapping into the power of asking, you are not having opportunities for your writing to be published and sold.

For example, if you want more reviews on Amazon for your books, are you consistently asking people if they are willing to read your book and write a review? It's been proven that a steady stream of reviews on Amazon (even if your book has been out a while) helps your book to sell even more copies. I understand it is important to get over 20 Amazon reviews (if possible) and 50 reviews is another benchmark. And when it comes to these reviews, I've often found willing people—but they haven't posted their review. Part of the process is to return to these individuals and make sure they have the book and remind them about the review. I understand there is a lot to read and write about since new books are being released into the market every day.

With the sheer volume of books entering the marketplace every day, it is a challenge for authors to get book reviews. Write a great book. Produce a great book (design and production is important) then finally take action to get your book reviewed. I've seen a number of books that have well-done production, great endorsements and zero or few reviews. The details are important and I encourage you to take an active role on this process of getting book reviews.

Why I Give Away Books—And You Should Too

If you have a published book, you have a powerful tool in your arsenal. I hate to admit it but when I entered publishing years ago, I was tight with my books. Each time I gave away a book, I was thinking about what that book cost for me to purchase it. As the years have passed, I've become less cautious about the actual cost and more aware of the way books can help others. In this section, I want to give you some reasons to give away your books.

At a recent Morgan James author event in Nashville, I asked one of the authors for her business card. She didn't have one. Immediately she said, "Why don't I give you a book and I will write my website into my book?" Your book can be the perfect business card in that situation. This author has been around publishing many years. I'm certain she had no idea that I've written hundreds of Amazon reviews. I gratefully received her book and carried the book home. A week or so later, I read the book cover to cover. It was excellent and I wrote a short book review on Amazon and Goodreads. While this author had recently launched her book, she only had eight book reviews. My short review helped her add to this number and I told others about my review through a short tweet with the book on Twitter.

To be realistic, I understand that my response to the gift of a book is not your normal response—but you can suggest readers post a review on Amazon and Goodreads as you hand them your book. Simply from the power of your suggestion, some people will do it.

At the same event, another Morgan James author asked for a copy of my *Billy Graham* book. I pulled it out, autographed it and handed it to her. She promised to read it and write a review. Each time I discover a new review, it gives me an opportunity to tell others about this review on social media (Twitter, Facebook, LinkedIn, etc.). Marketing people understand a reader has to hear about your book seven or eight times (at least) before they decide to purchase your book. With each new review, you should seize the opportunity on social media to tell others. That exposure is building and adding to the time when that reader will purchase your book.

Here's several reasons to give away your books:

1. **Books change the lives of readers.** I know books change lives because years ago, I read a book that changed my life. You can watch me tell my story about the book in this short video (http://youtu.be/7P9KC90QcsU).

2. **Books in the right hands can help you promote your book.** Be watching for other readers and others who write reviews of books and give them a book. Also be generous with people who are in the media to give them copies of your book. Be prepared to give away your books. Carry the books in your car or briefcase and use them as you have the opportunity.

Finally, follow up with the individuals after you have given away your book. In your follow-up note, tell them what you would like them to do and make it easy for them to do it. If you aren't telling them (asking), they may not think of the idea on their own. Your follow-up note can be simple saying something like:

"I'd appreciate it if you could leave your honest review of my *Billy Graham* book in three places:

Amazon: **http://amzn.to/1gYtzbx**
Barnes & Noble.com: **http://bit.ly/1zLviz6**
Goodreads: **http://bit.ly/1rTDzYB** Your review will be a huge help."

Notice several details about my follow-up note. It was short, specific and I gave them the actual links to go to the right location online to leave their review. You can use my follow-up note as a template for your own actions with others.

If you are generous with your books (give them away) and tell people what you need from them, many of them will be glad to help you.

Four Reasons Book Reviews Make A Difference

Recently I noticed a short video from one of my author friends. She was headed to a bookstore for an event and book signing. As I watched her video, it was news for me the author even had a book. I went over to Amazon, the largest online bookstore on the planet, and typed her name into the search tool. In an instant, I found several new books which had released about two months earlier.

Immediately I noticed the incomplete Amazon listing. The page had no book cover, no detailed information about the book *and* no book reviews. I hope this author had gathered a good crowd at her book signing (which can be lonely experiences). I'm still amazed at the lack of reviews because this person "should" have known the importance of book reviews on Amazon but had zero reviews. It sends out the wrong message when people view the book on Amazon. I want to highlight four reasons book reviews make a difference.

1. **Shows Others Are Reading Your Book.** When I go to the book page on Amazon and it has no reviews (or only three or four), it makes me wonder if others are buying and reading the book.

Sometimes there are many reviews on the Amazon page for another reason. For example, journalist Megyn Kelly released her book, *Settle for More*. I listened to the audio book. Two or three days after the book released, I went to the Amazon page, there were over 200 reviews. Many of the reviews were one or two stars and obviously from people who disliked Kelly and had not read or heard any of her book. Amazon has recently cracked down on these reviews. I reviewed the audio book and posted it on Amazon but my review was not "a verified purchase" since I didn't buy the book on Amazon. I looked for my Five Star review of

Kelly's book and Amazon has removed it—the first time this has happened to me that I know about. With all of the controversy tied to this book, I can see how removing reviews which were not purchased directly on Amazon was a way to thin out the reviews.

2. **Prove You are Promoting Your Book.** It's a first step to publish your book (traditional or self-published). But every author needs to be promoting his or her book. If you have reviews, (positive and negative but honest), it is proof of your marketing efforts.

3. **Encourage Additional Book Sales.** Millions of customers are buying books every day on Amazon, Barnes & Noble, Christian Book.com and other websites. Reviews help those customer's buying decisions.

4. **Show You Have On-going Readers**. Maybe your book has been out for a while. Is it getting new book reviews? If so, these reviews are proof that people continue to gain value from your book. A few weeks ago, Brent Sampson, founder of Outskirts Press reviewed my *Jumpstart Your Publishing Dreams*. While *Jumpstart Your Publishing Dreams* has been out for several years, a new review shows readers the book is continuing to help others. As you read or listen to books, *write reviews* on Amazon and Goodreads. It's a simple way you can support others through writing honest reviews.

Myth Buster Action (MBA): Marketing your book is your responsibility. Create business cards and bookmarks and always have your book with you to sell it or show it. Also make a decision to write honest reviews about any book you read or hear.

Chapter 10

Myth Ten

The Life of a Writer is Glamorous

Whether you have never published a book or published many books, you may have this concept that authors have a magical life. They get to travel, attend amazing events and talk with well-known people about their book. Bestselling authors must have a wonderful life because they have sold so many books. This concept that the writing life is glamorous is another publishing myth.

In my 20+ years in publishing, there are remarkable moments. I want to begin this chapter with a couple of these moments. Early in my writing career, I attended the

Mount Hermon Christian Writers Conference which is one of the longest continual events of this type. Located in the California redwoods, the event is known for their premier faculty and facility. At the end of this event, they give out some writer awards. During one of these early conferences, to my complete surprise, I was given an award for the Writer of the Year. The moment was outstanding to me because it was the only writer award I've ever received. For the majority of writers, it is rare to receive a public reward or honor.

Fast forward years later, I was writing a book with the leading African American in Promise Keepers, Bishop Philip Porter. At the time, Promise Keepers was the fastest-growing men's movement in America. I worked with a New York literary agent and we crafted a book proposal that launched a bidding war between two large publishers. It was an exciting moment in my publishing life to sign a book contract with a six-figure advance. I worked hard on the writing for this book and it was published. Yet the truth is the book was unsuccessful and did not sell for several reasons. The publisher never showed the cover to Bishop Porter before it was published. Bishop Porter's picture filled the cover of this book but he did not like it. He disliked it to the point of not promoting the book and it did not sell. The publisher took this book out of print after six months. How is that for a glamorous writing life? Most of those out-of-print books were destroyed—the truth of what happens to many of these books.

Met Former President Jimmy Carter

"We can't say anything about it," my literary attorney and writer friend Sallie Randolph began. "But President Jimmy Carter and his wife Rosalynn are going to be at our member luncheon tomorrow."

I was in New York City for the annual conference of the American Society of Journalists and Authors (ASJA), the leading nonfiction writers group in the nation and originally known as the Society of Magazine Writers. Each year, the organization holds a large public conference on a Saturday in a hotel in New York City. Before this public conference, the ASJA has a much smaller member day meeting in the same location. One of our members had written a book with Rosalynn Carter and the authors were going to be given an award from the Society. The award winners were invited to attend the member luncheon and the Carters had accepted the invitation. There would be about 200 members and special guests at this luncheon.

While Sallie and I were not sitting at the table of honor with the former president and his wife, we figured out where the secret service would be sitting and were able to sit at that table. My business book, *Lessons from the Pit, A Successful Veteran of the Chicago Mercantile Exchange Shows Executives How to Thrive in a Competitive Environment* which I wrote for Joe Leininger, had just been released and I had a copy in my briefcase. During the meal, I asked a secret service agent when I could give President Carter a copy of my book. He said, "Do it right now because we're going to eat, speak, and leave."

With his permission, I walked over to the former president, introduced myself, and gave him a copy of my book which was published from B & H Publishing Group (formerly Broadman & Holman). I knew Broadman had been one of Jimmy Carter's publishers and he would be familiar with the company. He was interested in the topic of my book and mentioned his son, Chip, had traded at the Chicago Mercantile.

As the meal concluded, the program began, the Carters spoke to the audience, and then quietly slipped out of the room—the president carrying one book out of that meeting—mine. It was a great experience to have met a former President and spend a few minutes with him.

I've interviewed more than 150 bestselling authors in many different settings. I've been inside the professional baseball locker of the San Diego Padres and been one of the few journalists who has interviewed bestselling author and pastor Chuck Swindoll. During our lunch, Chuck told me, "There are no heroes in the Body of Christ. We are all like a bunch of guys in the back of a pick-up trying to get our stuff together." The experience of meeting various bestselling authors and hearing their stories has been enriching to my life but is not glamorous.

The reality is writing books is hard work and selling books is even harder. From my experience there is often little glamour attached to such work. I've never met a book author who didn't want to sell more copies of their work. It doesn't matter if they are published through one of the largest publishers or Podunk Press (I don't believe there is such a small publisher named Podunk Press but maybe, since there are many of them).

If you bring up the topic of selling more books, almost every author has a story about something they tried yet failed to work. Often these stories are filled with the author blaming someone else for the lack of sales. They blame:

- their publisher
- their publicist
- their agent
- their editor
- the wrong title
- the wrong cover
- the missing endorsements
- _____ you name it

It's rare that I hear the author blame the real culprit: themselves. Yes, it's hard to admit but it is the first step toward selling more books and understanding who bears the true responsibility for selling books—the author.

Many authors long to have their book appear on the bestseller list. For some authors they equate getting on the bestseller list as their benchmark of success for their book.

Over ten years ago, I read Michael Korda's *Making the List, a Cultural History of the American Bestseller 1900–1999*. Korda at the time was the Editor-in-Chief at Simon and Schuster, one of the largest publishers. If you haven't read this book, I highly recommend it.

In the introduction, Korda writes, "The bestseller list is therefore neither as predictable nor as dominating as its critics make it out to be. Plenty of strange books get onto the list and stay there for a long time…at least half of the books on any given list are there to the immense surprise and puzzlement of their publishers. That's why publishers find it so hard to repeat their success—half the time they can't figure out how it happened in the first place." (Page xv) I love his honesty. There is no magic bullet and it is different for every book. The author is key.

Some books start slow and steadily sell then catapult in sales. Other books begin strong then sales drop to nothing. There is no consistent pattern.

My encouragement is for you to keep experimenting with different methods to sell your book. Each author has a different experience. Recently I spoke with an author who had sold 8,000 to 10,000 copies of his self-published books. He had held over 300 book signings for his book. For many authors book signings have yielded almost nothing but not for this author. He regularly speaks at schools and service clubs and even AARP meetings.

Good Writing Takes Hours of Practice

Because we have computers and can produce stories, everyone assumes writing is easy. From my experience, any skill (including writing) takes hours of practice to become excellent. For example, one of the most successful basketball players of all time is Kobe Bryant, the winner of five NBA championships and two Olympic Gold Medals. He accomplished this success through deliberate practice. Bryant was on the 2012 Team USA. One of the trainers, Robert tells about his first experience with Bryant who started his conditioning work at 4:30 am. He shot baskets for several hours, then did conditioning work for the next hour, then made 800 jump shots between 7 am and 11 am. Bryant was a skilled professional but took nothing for granted in his practice and work outs. His work showed because Bryant knew how to grind then grind some more. This type of effort in sports is generally lost in the writing world. There are hours of work and effort behind the scenes that no one sees but is necessary to achieve success.

The Hidden Costs of Publishing

There are many things in the world of publishing which simply add to the cost and effort to happen but are never documented or talked about. In many ways, these elements become some of the hidden costs of publishing. In some ways publishing is like an iceberg. We can see the top on the water but don't realize all that is below the surface. In this section I wanted to tell you about a couple of these hidden costs, and give you some tools and basic principles for your own writing life.

People look at my large twitter following (over 200,000) and would like to have that ability to influence and touch others. Yet are you willing to do the work to build that following? I've written in my blog about the five actions I take every day on Twitter. (https://bit.ly/22eu5vS) I use a program called Refollow to help automate this effort. Sometimes the program does not work. Every day I can use it to quickly follow 800 people in my target market. Then I can also use this program to unfollow people who have not followed me back. Some of these people I followed years ago and I use Refollow to automatically unfollow them. This unfollow process involves clicking and unfollowing each person—up to 1,000 a day.

Recently several times the program got stuck. The only way I've found to get it working is to leave the site (stopping the process) and to begin it again (and re-clicking all those times). Other times error messages are thrown up on my screen. Maybe Twitter has blocked the unfollow process or something else. These stops and starts amount to some substantial time with zero or little results. Yet I persist because I understand it is all part of the process of continuing to build my audience and presence in the market. I use these tools consistently day after day. I also tweet good content throughout the day. People who tweet once a week or once a day in general do not have a large number of followers on Twitter. Instead I tweet 12-15 times each day with different content.

Over the years, I've created a number of online information products like *Blogging for Bucks* (http://bucksforblog.com/) or my *Write a Book Proposal course* (http://bit.ly/wbkpro). I've automated many of these products through autoresponders and other tools. Each of these products include my 100% Love it Or Leave It Guarantee. If the buyer isn't satisfied in a period of time, they can send an email and ask for a refund. This guarantee is a key part of selling products online and it is rare that someone will ask for a refund. One email arrived at a time when I was challenged with other things—yet I took the time to make the refund. Carrying through with your promises is a key part of having an online business and successfully selling products online. It doesn't make it simple or easy.

Here's some basic principles for every writer to understand beyond the hidden costs of publishing:

❖ Be aware the costs are there and keep going in spite of them

❖ Automate when you can. Invest in tools like Hootsuite, Manage Flitter and Refollow. They allow you to continually grow your presence and save time

❖ Grow in your craft of writing, attending conferences, taking online courses and reading books.

❖ Understand timing is critical and yet often out of your control. I've had authors who have looked for an agent for years (not found it) then return to Morgan James and ask if they can sign our book contract. I've had it happen numerous times. An author signed recently who I have been speaking with off and on for three years about her book.

❖ Take the long view of success and keep doing the little things and working to promote you and your writing.

Over and over I speak with authors who continue promoting yet have stopped telling their publisher about their promotion (big mistake in my view). The publisher is going to assume they are not promoting and has stopped talking about the author with their sales team and the sales team to the bookstores since it is tied together. Yet if the author continues to promote *and* tells the publisher, then the communication and promotion to the bookstores can continue. Consistent communication matters.

No little elves come out and write this material for us. We have to be the ones to tell the stories and complete the work. Take proactive steps to learn a new skill or try some new way to sell books. It doesn't matter if your book is brand new or has been in print for a while. Keep the experimentation going until you hit the elements which work for your book.

 Myth Buster Action (MBA): Be proactive and take regular steps in the right direction. Be realistic rather than believe the myths.

Don't Miss the 11ᵗʰ Publishing Myth

In the final stages of this book, a publishing colleague suggested I was missing another myth. There are many more publishing myths than the 10 which are explained in this book.

I have written an extra chapter and here's where you can get immediate access:

www.terrylinks.com/11thmyth

<u>Please don't miss this important information.</u>

A Final Note about
10 Publishing Myths

I hope you have found the stories and information in *10 Publishing Myths* enlightening for your writing life and your dreams about publishing. I'd love to hear from you so hope we can connect through email or LinkedIn or any number of other ways.

For more insights, be sure to follow my blog on the Writing Life at: http://thewritinglife.ws and you can subscribe to it on email at: http://bit.ly/1F9r3Ro

Finally, I'd appreciate an honest review of the book on Amazon: https://amzn.to/2YVxkvC

Or Barnes & Noble: www.barnesandnoble.com

Or Goodreads: www.goodreads.com

If you are unsure what to write for a review, then use this Reader Book Review Form for Nonfiction to give you some help: http://terrylinks.com/nrbrf (used with permission from Sandra Beckwith at Build Book Buzz). I know it takes time and energy to write a review and ahead of time I'd like to thank you for your efforts.

Acknowledgements

Writing a book is a solitary action where an individual tells stories and give information in words on paper (and on the screen). From my years in publishing, the best type of publishing involves a village of people and is a consensus building process. Do you have the right title? Have you selected the right cover? These details are just two of the multitude of decisions involved in the publishing process. I acknowledge these decisions did not happen alone but with a team of people.

Centuries ago King Solomon wrote, "There is nothing new under the sun." Ecclesiastes 1:9 While these pages have some creative spin on the contents, I want to acknowledge the details and the stories come from many different sources.

Insights have come from reading books, sitting in lectures, interviewing bestselling authors and dozens of other ways. I want to express my appreciation and gratitude for each of these teachers in my life. This work and all of my books stand on the foundation of these teachers.

I want to thank my long-time journalism friend and editor, Nancy Caine, for her work to improve the editorial content of this book.

I want to acknowledge and express appreciation to the Morgan James Publishing team. These skilled professionals do remarkable work every day and this book would not be possible without their input and expertise. Instead of listing many names and neglecting to include them, I want to simply acknowledge every one of them.

Finally, my appreciation and gratitude to Christine for listening to countless stories about books and publishing and being my wife and partner in this work. Thank you.

About the Author

Terry Whalin has loved books since his mother read *And to Think That I Saw It on Mulberry* Street (the first Dr. Seuss book). He has worked both sides of the editorial desk—as an editor and a writer. He worked as a magazine editor and his magazine work has appeared in more than 50 publications. A former literary agent, Terry is an Acquisitions Editor at Morgan James Publishing.

He has written more than 60 books through traditional publishers in a wide range of topics from children's books to biographies to co-authored books. Several of Terry's books have sold over 100,000 copies.

Terry's book, *Jumpstart Your Publishing Dreams, Insider Secrets to Skyrocket Your Success* (Morgan James Publishing) is packed with insight. His most recent book is *Billy Graham, A Biography of America's Greatest Evangelist* (Morgan James Publishing). Also Terry has an innovative online training course to help authors effectively connect with literary agents and editors called *Write A Book Proposal*. Terry is a popular speaker and teacher at numerous writers' conferences and an active member of the American Society of Journalists and Authors. He lives near Denver, Colorado and has an active following on twitter (@terrywhalin).

CPSIA information can be obtained
at www.ICGtesting.com
Printed in the USA
BVHW031310171119
564075BV00001B/30/P

9 781642 794526